T0407415

THE DISINHERITED MAJORITY

THE DISINHERITED MAJORITY

Capital Questions—Piketty and Beyond

◆ ◆ ◆

By Charles Derber

with Interludes by

Juliet B. Schor, Chuck Collins, Josh Hoxie, and Yale Magrass

and

a brief interview with Thomas Piketty

Paradigm Publishers
Boulder • London

Copyright © 2015 Paradigm Publishers

Published in the United States by Paradigm Publishers, 5589 Arapahoe Avenue, Boulder, CO 80303 USA.

Paradigm Publishers is the trade name of Birkenkamp & Company, LLC, Dean Birkenkamp, President and Publisher.

Library of Congress Cataloging-in-Publication Data

Derber, Charles.
    The disinherited majority : capital questions—Piketty and beyond / Charles Derber.
        pages cm
    Includes bibliographical references and index.
    ISBN 978-1-61205-831-3 (hardcover : alk. paper)—
    ISBN 978-1-61205-832-0 (pbk. : alk. paper)—
    ISBN 978-1-61205-834-4 (library ebook)—
    ISBN 978-1-61205-833-7 (consumer ebook)
    1. Inheritance and succession.   2. Capitalism.   3. Income distribution.
4. Wealth.   5. Social justice.   6. Social history—21st century.   I. Title.
    HB715.D47 2015
    332'.041—dc23

                                                                2014035151

Printed and bound in the United States of America on acid-free paper that meets the standards of the American National Standard for Permanence of Paper for Printed Library Materials.

19 18 17 16 15   1 2 3 4 5

CONTENTS

PREFACE

CAPITAL QUESTIONS AND THE
DISINHERITED MAJORITY: A MAP

I n this book, I offer an analysis of society in the twenty-first century. This is not a modest undertaking, but I have a lot of help, starting with the book by Thomas Piketty, *Capital in the Twenty-First Century*.[1] His work took the world by storm when published in 2014. It opened up a window into our future—one that is both brilliantly illuminating and deeply alarming for any person concerned with human rights, equality, and social justice.

Piketty's book is a jumping-off place—a launching pad—for this volume. Piketty is raising a set of what I call "capital questions" about capitalism itself. His capital questions spur a very big conversation, one starting with Adam Smith and Karl Marx, about the kind of economic and political order that we have constructed, one in which the principle of inheritance—and trillions of dollars of inherited wealth—may largely shape our future.

But Piketty is opening rather than closing the conversation. My purpose here is to make my own small contribution to where I think that conversation about capital questions—and the political action that must follow—should go. I draw with great appreciation from Piketty, but we must move considerably beyond him to get to answers that will preserve the dignity of billions of people, whom I call the disinherited majority. The disinherited majority makes up most people in the United States and in the world, but it is largely excluded from wealth, power, and the rights to a dignified life. This is a book about how to remake the world of, by, and for that majority.

Here is a brief map explaining how I have organized the book. My introduction starts with a short summary of my own main thesis: about the twenty-first-century crisis of the disinherited majority and how to respond to it. In the rest of the introduction, I summarize Piketty's work because it is the catalyst and "instrument" for offering you my own analysis. You do not need to have read Piketty to read and enjoy this book, but you are advised to read my introduction (which summarizes Piketty's main findings) if you haven't read him, and probably even if you have.

Following the introduction is the main part of the book, fourteen chapters, each of which takes up one "capital question" or theme. Each chapter begins with a cluster of questions on a key theme. In each chapter, I offer a summary of Piketty's perspective, examine the flood of commentary that he has elicited, and then offer my own way of reframing and diving deeper into the theme in question. My approach is to push beyond the economic framework that Piketty offers, probing much further into the social and political questions that Piketty says are integral to understanding the economy. Piketty is a blunt critic of the limits of his own economics profession, making clear that the study of economics is barren without an equal dose of history, sociology, and politics. But having been trained as an economist, Piketty himself does not offer the strong social and political analysis—and medicine—that he argues, correctly, that we desperately need. My hope is to offer a deeper diagnosis of the social and political illness—and glimpses of the twenty-first-century social and political medicine that might start the healing.

Two other elements are part of my map. One is brief commentaries by individuals whose views I deeply respect. Piketty has helped stir the conversation that I want to pursue, but it will take a vast community of scholars, students, and ordinary people to move the conversation in the right direction. To underscore that this is a conversation for everyone, I have included a small number of voices other than mine, who are already thinking on capital questions and working for the disinherited majority. Their voices in the book, highlighted as brief interludes spaced through the work, will make clear that we need a conversation rather than a monologue.

On the same theme, I have put discussion questions for you, the reader, after each of the fourteen capital questions. If it takes a village to undertake this inquiry, it is you, and all your friends, family, and workplace or neighborhood colleagues, who must participate in the conversation. By adding these discussion questions, I am once again trying to say that no single person—certainly not just myself—can help us find our path into a more equal, sustainable, and democratic twenty-first century. That is the work of all of us.

ACKNOWLEDGMENTS

L et me first thank Thomas Piketty, for writing *Capital in the Twenty-First Century*. I wrote this work to continue and help reframe the conversation that Piketty has catalyzed. I want to thank Piketty for his cooperation and willingness to do an interview with me.

I extend many thanks also to my publisher and friend, Dean Birkenkamp, founder and director of Paradigm Publishers. He has supported me generously in every step of the development of this book. Dean played an important role in helping frame the argument and organize the various parts of the book. He is the publisher that every author dreams of finding.

I want to thank my friend and colleague, Yale Magrass, for helping me develop the core theme of the book on capitalism as a society based on both caste and class. He has written his own brilliant commentary about capitalism as a caste society, included in this volume. I also thank him for taking the time to go closely over the entire manuscript and offer his comments.

I also want to thank other contributors who added their own voice in commentaries, including my friends and colleagues Chuck Collins, Julie Schor, and Josh Hoxie.

Thanks also to all the folks at Paradigm who were so helpful. And thanks to my always supportive friends and colleagues, David Karp and John Williamson. A special thanks also to Elena, whose keen intellect and love lit the way forward.

INTRODUCTION

PIKETTY FOR THE PEOPLE: CASTE, CLASS, AND THE DISINHERITED MAJORITY

With the landmark success of his book *Capital in the Twenty-First Century*, Thomas Piketty has spurred a new global conversation about money and morality in a troubled capitalist world. If we do not pursue that conversation, we may lose our hope to solve urgent problems of extreme inequality, dynastic wealth, and democratic collapse.

My goal is to help you participate as easily and enjoyably as possible in this intellectual and political adventure. Piketty himself says that his book is the beginning rather than the end of the conversation. Indeed, there is much to be learned from his work, but even more to be pursued beyond where he goes. This book offers my own perspective on how to interpret and move forward, as a nation and a world, from his work. I am writing to advance the thinking both of those who have read Piketty and also those who have not read his work but want to be literate participants in the conversation he has helped accelerate.

Most of this introduction is devoted to a summary of Piketty's main arguments. But I want, first, to give you a brief view of why I think his book is important and why and how we can take his ideas and move beyond them to solve our twenty-first-century crises.

Piketty's work is a diagnosis of what the twenty-first century—our economics, politics, and society—is likely to look like. What is most fascinating is his view that we can see the future most clearly by looking far back into our past. Social commentaries today emphasize how unique our future will be, hinting that we best forget history and become futurists, intrepid explorers of the unknown and totally new. But Piketty's argument is that we need to look back to see the future.

The best futurists will be the best historians, those who truly understand the past.

I think he is right—and that most of us, including those who flooded the Internet and blogs and book review pages with reviews of Piketty—have failed to understand the implications. They are quite revolutionary.

Piketty is an economist—he calls himself a "political economist"—focused on our economic and political arrangements. He has chosen inequality, now extreme especially in America but also in much of the world—as his main topic. He looks in a new way at the system of capitalism that produces it. As I explain later, his view is that extreme inequality is a sign of "perfectly operating" markets and a defining attribute of almost all capitalist eras over the centuries.

This opens us up to new "capital questions" about capitalism, exploding deeply held beliefs in the United States. We equate American capitalism with the American Dream. Capitalism has made America the land of opportunity, a new and "exceptionalist" system in which everyone has a chance to succeed through hard work and merit—and where most will prosper. We have broken the mold, by breaking with the rigid class systems of Old Europe and moving beyond societies polarized between lords and serfs, between wealthy merchants and impoverished workers.

That Old European world, going back even before the beginnings of capitalism in the late Middle Ages, was a world of caste. Caste is a status you are born into and cannot change. In America today caste is largely associated with your race or gender. In the ancient European world of caste, you were also defined by biology, the "blood" or essence you inherited from your parents and their parents, and ordained by God. A caste society is a never-changing social world in which the principle of inheritance rules. It is also a cruel world, for the disinherited majority of serfs or peasants were forever chained to their tiny plot of land and excluded in perpetuity from wealth or power.[1] Even Karl Marx celebrated the rise of capitalism because it appeared to break that cruel system of caste and open up opportunities for all. Marx saw this new system as creating its own harsh divisions, but they were based on class rather than caste, and opened up at least new ideals of greater mobility and prosperity for all. The caste world was buried under the enormous productive machinery of the new industrial capitalism engine.

But Piketty suddenly tells us the world of caste has not disappeared at all. In fact, he argues that caste (while he never uses the word) is reappearing in twenty-first-century capitalism, and may well define the coming century as deeply as it did Old Europe. And there is more. This is not something new about capitalism, which never actually buried caste at all. Nor did it ever discard the principle of inheritance that it claimed to replace with the principle of work and merit—and the promise of wealth and opportunity for all.

The capitalist world, in other words, has always been a world of caste. In this book, I stare into the face of that poorly understood reality, which has enormous implications for our thinking and politics.

Piketty himself, as well as the flood of commentators responding to him, have discussed Piketty's idea of "patrimonial capitalism," in which dynastic wealth is concentrated in tiny upper classes that the Occupy Wall Street Movement called the 1%, whose children will inherit great fortunes. But Piketty and those who have helped explore his message do not deeply explore the idea of caste. My aim in this book is to shift the conversation to a full understanding of the intellectual and political implications of living in a caste-based world, keeping in mind that it is one completely intertwined with class divisions growing ever more severe.

Let me just briefly introduce a few of my ideas and implications that I highlight in this book. One is that we need to focus deeply on the meaning of caste. In the United States, it has largely biological definitions, associated with race, gender, and sexual orientation. These biological castes play a major role in American life and have generated civil rights, feminist, and sexual-orientation movements to overcome caste discrimination and oppression.

But Piketty's work suggests we are defining caste wrongly—or incompletely. Yes, there remain biological castes of great importance. But the twenty-first century will be a world in which economic castes are as real and important as biological castes. The 1% and the 99% are increasingly emerging as economic castes, whose inheritance (or disinheritance, the condition of the majority and the fate of much of the 99%) defines them permanently. They will never enjoy either wealth or power, a tragic consequence but one not new by any means, since capitalism has routinely operated, with some important exceptions, by the logic of caste.

A second implication, yet to be fully explained, is that caste and class are melding in America. The dominant social categories in the United States are "caste classes." They have attributes of both caste and class. And the Piketty analysis suggests that the twenty-first-century world may be scarred by the worst features of a permanent entanglement of class and caste, particularly if people do not become conscious of themselves as members of "caste classes" whose fate depends on acting together to liberate themselves from two intertwined forms of power and exclusion.

Again, these are not new realities, since capitalism has almost always organized itself around entangled class and caste, even though this has not been widely understood. But beyond these realities is a third more hopeful possibility, also yet to be widely discussed. A system organized around caste and class power invites a new kind of politics. This is one in which "caste classes" operate to open up the chains of both the caste and class worlds, and bring together previously separate culture movements of caste and economic movements of class.

The United States has had strong caste movements, especially the civil rights movements of people of color and feminist movements of women. But these movements have focused on overcoming caste discrimination while ignoring the larger class movement. Their goals have been largely to integrate people into the larger capitalist system, not to reform or overturn it. I will show how this has severely weakened the ability of caste movements to deal with their majorities of economically disadvantaged members.

At the same time, class movements have been weakened by their own failures to recognize the intertwining of caste and class discrimination. It has led working-class movements, traditionally led by white men, to separate themselves from and often resist the rise of biological caste movements. This has divided the labor movement by race and gender and deeply weakened the working class as a change agent in the United States.

The future of US and global politics depends on understanding caste and class realities, and creating a strong and liberating politics that flows from that new analysis. Piketty's work has opened up windows into this radical rethinking of our society, and I will start by showing how his analysis takes us on the first steps of this new intellectual and political journey. But I will also show the limitations of his work, which has largely failed to illuminate this road not taken. The consequences have led to needless suffering by millions of people.

I also suggest that once we have grasped the full meaning of caste, and we have recognized the caste and class realities of capitalism that we have long denied, there is hope to avoid the worst possibilities of the twenty-first-century nightmare that Piketty deems possible, if not probable. With some luck, we can find a new politics that offers true possibilities of empowerment and dignity for the disinherited majority.

I should add, finally, that my argument draws on two different "voices" in Piketty's work, which I dub Piketty 1 and Piketty 2. Piketty 1 is a fairly conventional Keynesian economist, who has used a pioneering method to open up the historical discussion of caste and class while staying largely within a traditional economics framework. Piketty 2 is a progressive human rights thinker and advocate, who realizes that the study of economics needs to centrally integrate social and political ideas. But Piketty 2's own politics are not visionary enough—or at least not spelled out enough in his book with the necessary social and political analysis—to show how the disinherited majority can gain equal rights and dignity.

In this book, I try to show how the hidden debate between the two Pikettys helps sharpen the new national conversation we now need. I also show why we need to move beyond not just Piketty 1 but also Piketty 2, with a more in-depth view of the politics of caste and class. I argue that we need political movements that ripple up from the grass roots to challenge the 1%, through which the disinherited majority can develop a new politics that takes us beyond the shackles of class and caste in the twenty-first century.

Having offered this glimpse of my own thinking, I want to summarize Piketty's work itself. If you have already read his book and digested his argument fully, you may want to skip the rest of this introduction, and move directly to the main part of this book. But if you have not read Piketty in his entirety, or want to learn more now how I interpret him, read on. I summarize here his basic thesis and explain the basic outline of his book, which is divided into four parts. First, I give a capsule summary of his main argument and how he approaches his subject, explained in his own introduction. Then, I move on to highlight briefly the key ideas in the four parts of his book.

In his introduction, Piketty puts forward his main argument. It turns on its head both conventional economics and the "common sense" underlying American beliefs in capitalism and the American Dream.

Here's Piketty's thesis. We live in a capitalist system hurtling toward ever more extreme inequality in the twenty-first century. Piketty has collected an encyclopedia of data showing that severe inequality has been a defining characteristic of Western capitalism for most of the past three hundred years. Only one period in the United States, during the mid-twentieth century from roughly 1932 to 1980, gave rise to greater equality. The forces for "divergence"—Piketty's term for rising inequality—are potent, and the prospects of defeating them in the twenty-first century "are not heartening."[2] That is because inequality is programmed into markets. Piketty says, "The main force of divergence in my theory has nothing to do with any market imperfection. Quite the contrary: the more perfect the capital market (in the economist's sense), the more likely" that extreme inequality will arise.[3] Piketty discredits at the outset the conventional assumption, based on the work of the mid-twentieth-century American economist Simon Kuznets, that capitalism creates over time a growth tide "lifting all boats."[4] Piketty's data suggest the opposite. Twenty-first-century New America will likely resemble Old Europe, the era described by great nineteenth-century European novelists such as Honore de Balzac and Jane Austen. In that world, great dynastic fortunes dominated a rigid class society, and the majority was disinherited, excluded from wealth and power.

Piketty's images of Old Europe—which he offers by taking us on lovely journeys through the novels of writers like Balzac and Austen—bring us to the second part of his thesis: we are moving toward a society so unequal that it will be governed by a 1% born into wealth and aristocratic privilege. In Old Europe, most people lived a lifetime of hard work that left them with crumbs. Only the very rich, living off their inheritances, could lead a high or dignified life.

Even Karl Marx welcomed the coming of capitalism because he accepted its claims that it would end the Old World's feudal caste system—a world in which rich and poor were born into their station and stayed there for life. In its place, capitalism would create class divisions, also deeply divisive but offering the majority at least the idea that they had the right to work to make a better life.

Piketty sees the return of a caste-based or patrimonial capitalism, clearly visible in eighteenth- and nineteenth-century European capitalism and in American capitalism today and going forward. The 1% inherits; the majority is disinherited; and class becomes caste. This raises questions about all our basic assumptions: that capitalism has unleashed basic freedoms to move up, that hard work will help the talented move forward, that birth does not determine your station for life, and that the markets themselves will raise the worthy up and eventually ensure the promise of the American Dream.

Piketty's is not a picture of twenty-first-century America that most of us would welcome, except perhaps the wealthiest Americans. It punctures so many ruling myths that the disinherited majority itself may refuse to believe it. But Piketty marshals so much evidence that it is difficult to dismiss him, and most readers will feel the need to see whether the argument is true, and if so, what can be done to turn a terrible forecast into a sunnier future.

But how did Piketty even get to the point of raising the question of inequality and the future of capitalism? This is a story in itself, and he recounts much of it in his introduction.

Piketty starts with a stark challenge to his own discipline: that professional economics can't help us understand the real economy. He doesn't entirely dismiss academic economics—after all, he was trained in it and you'll find a lot of it in his book. But he argues that professional economics has moved away from its roots in nineteenth-century "political economy," the kind of big thinking pioneered by Adam Smith, David Ricardo, and Karl Marx. Political economy argued that the economy is so intertwined with history, social values and institutions, and political power that it makes no sense to separate out the study of economics from the broader study of history and society.

Piketty left the United States for France because he felt he couldn't do his political economy in America. The heart of his method is historical—his book is a meticulous look at the distribution of wealth over three hundred years. To do economic history seems almost quaint in America, and although my own father, Milton Derber, was an economic historian, that approach died with his generation of New Deal economists. Today, you will not find a single economic historian in most American departments of economics.

History is at the heart of classical political economy. We should be grateful that Piketty had the courage of his intellectual convictions. He announces in his introduction that his book will present a vast collection of data—assembled by a distinguished team of economists across the world over the past two decades—on the distribution of wealth and income in more than twenty countries over one to three centuries, depending on the nation. His "big data" is drawn partly from income tax records and estate tax records that took enormous ingenuity to collect and standardize. It is almost certainly the biggest such historical data set ever collected. Most analysts agree that it is the strength of his meticulous historical research on centuries of wealth and inequality that gave his work credibility and helped his findings go viral across the world.

Piketty announces that he will go forward by looking backward. His political economy approach is a return to Adam Smith and Karl Marx.[5] Along with other major eighteenth- and nineteenth-century social thinkers they were economic historians, as well as sociologists and moral philosophers. They well understood that the economy was a subset of society and that social mores and political power shape the economy as much as the "laws" of supply and demand, which themselves turn out to be social constructions rather than anything like laws of physics.

Piketty argues from the beginning that economics is history, sociology, politics, and economics all wrapped up together like the intertwined strands of DNA. Here, he explicitly evokes Smith and Marx, among others, to say if you want to understand capitalism in the twenty-first century, you have to go back to the kind of work done in the nineteenth century. American universities will have to reinvent themselves to support the kind of work that Piketty has done, blasting big holes through the walls separating departments and bringing people together in new programs of capitalist studies or political economy to support useful work.

Piketty announces two other ways that he will go backward to see forward. First, he is going to put inequality and redistribution of wealth center stage, a subject today's economists have largely abandoned. "The economists of the nineteenth century deserve immense credit for placing the distributional question at the heart of economic analysis. . . . It is long since past the time when we should have put the question of inequality back at the center of economic analysis and begun asking questions first raised in the nineteenth century."[6]

To do that, though, Piketty has to look backward to an even bigger issue: capitalism itself! Piketty hinted this was his aim in his title: *Capital in the Twenty-First Century*. He knew that any literate reader would immediately be reminded of Marx, who made the critical study of capitalism his life work.

There is a conversation between Piketty and Marx that runs just beneath the surface—and sometimes becomes explicit. Both authors are fundamentally concerned with capitalism, its past and future as well as its morality. Piketty spends more than three of his first ten pages of his book on Marx, raising questions about capital accumulation and the capitalist apocalypse Marx imagined. Piketty argues that Marx was wrong about capitalist collapse, but he ends up describing a different kind of apocalypse as a real possibility.

Piketty thus subtly announces early on that capitalism is a topic back on the table—and is, in fact, the centerpiece of his book. He is looking for fundamental capitalist tendencies or laws, and he tells us in his introduction that he is going to apply a social and moral lens in doing so, particularly by looking at inequality. There is the implicit message that this book is a return to the largely abandoned nineteenth-century political economy focused on critical thinking about capitalism as a system, something that Occupy Wall Street shouted for but could not jump-start on its own.

Onward, then, to Parts 1 and 2, which set the table for his center-piece discussion of inequality in Part 3. In these first two sections, Piketty presents the basic concepts that allow him to analyze both inequality and the underlying laws of capitalism itself. His basic concepts are not entirely unfamiliar to economists, sociologists, or, in fact, any reader of the newspapers or Internet, but Piketty offers new and precise definitions of capital, income, and their historical evolution. In Parts 1 and 2 he uses them, among other things, to analyze the part of national income that goes to capital and the part going to labor, obviously both an economic and moral question, and one that Karl Marx himself famously made a subject of worldwide attention.

On his very first page, Piketty starts as Marx might have, focusing on a South African 2012 mining strike, in which thirty-four workers were killed for organizing to double their miserable wages. They died, Piketty says, because of the feverish intensity of the question of what is a just share of the division between profits (or return on capital) and wages. The miners struck because their "hopes for a more equitable distribution of income and a more democratic social order were dashed."[7] Just to be clear, Piketty puts the problem of Parts 1 and 2 this way: "What is the 'right' split between capital and labor? Can we be sure that an economy based on the 'free market' and private property always and everywhere leads to an optimal division, as if by magic? In an ideal society, how would one arrange the division between capital and labor?"[8] Here, Piketty is asking the question Marx saw key to any analysis of capitalism:

a question involving both economics and social justice. Marx predicted that capitalism would increasingly return more and more income to capital at the expense of labor, creating exploitation and injustice. He would certainly applaud—loudly—Piketty's argument that this question needs to be put center stage in the analysis of capitalism, especially when Piketty makes clear that professional economists are totally wrong-headed to assume that the capitalist markets themselves can be trusted to create a fair distribution. At least in this question, Piketty, who is trained as a Keynesian economist, is going back to some of the fundamentals of Marx.

The first concept Piketty presents is capital itself, which he defines as equivalent to wealth. This definition of capital would not have made Marx happy. Marx saw capital as the "means of production," the factory buildings, machinery, and tools used to produce things—or "factors of production." But Piketty includes in his idea of capital all the wealth that has nothing to do with production: people's homes; their cars; all other personal property. And he also includes gold, which is not typically used as a factor of production.[9] Marx saw such wealth outside of production as a distraction to any serious analysis of capital and capitalism, which is all about production, workers, and the struggle between workers and capitalists about who should own capital and control the economy.

Piketty disagrees. Personal property and gold are "a store of value." But they also can be used as a factor of production; for example, homes can become places of business, and gold becomes a productive factor in manufacturing jewelry. "Capital in all its forms," writes Piketty, "has always played a dual role, as both a store of value and a factor of production. I therefore decided that it was simpler not to impose a rigid distinction between wealth and capital."[10]

Piketty thus explains why he views capital as any asset that has value in a market. This shift in the idea of capital—from Marx's idea to Piketty's—may seem academic, but it has implications, leading Marx and Piketty in somewhat different directions, as I show later. But, you must absorb Piketty's definition of capital: "The total market value of everything owned by the residents and government of a given country at a given point in time, provided that it can be traded on some market."[11] Piketty's first two parts are all about what kind of wealth (meaning capital) exists in a society and how the amount of capital compares to the amount of income. Because when capital or wealth is very high compared to income, there are serious implications for equality and justice. Some of the next few paragraphs will seem a bit technical, but stay with me because Piketty's technical definitions are necessary to understand issues of social justice. It is not rocket science, and you can grasp it.

What is the definition of income? Again, Piketty is very precise: "National income is defined as the sum of all income available to the residents of a given country in a given year, regardless of the legal classification of that income."[12] Income can come from two sources: first from wages or income from labor and, second, from return on capital, such as stock dividends, rent from land, or interest from money in the bank.

The concepts of capital and income lead to a concept used all through his book: the ratio of capital to income, or the capital/income ratio. In most developed countries the capital/income ratio is about 5 or 6 to 1, meaning that the society's total value of wealth or stock of capital is five or six times the amount of the total income per year, so it would take five or six years of income to equal the wealth of a nation.

Why is any of this important? Piketty has already pointed out in his discussion of the miners killed in South Africa that they died to get a fairer distribution of income for their labor rather than see it go to capitalists. Escalating this deadly conflict to the national level, the miners would want to know what the capital/income ratio is because it helps define how a society is dividing income between capital and labor—and is a measure of social justice. A high capital/income ratio is a likely sign of serious inequality and injustice.

The rate of return on capital is a third big Piketty concept. It "measures the yield on capital over the course of a year regardless of its legal form (profits, rents, dividends, interest, royalties, capital gains etc.)."[13] Piketty denotes the rate of return on capital as r—and it is central to his book. A fourth big Piketty concept is g—or growth, defined by the rate of growth in the goods and services, or total income, of the society. We come back to growth in Part 3.

Once you know the capital/income ratio and r you can quickly compute capital's share in national income. That is what the miners died for: a more just share for their hard work that would reduce capital's share in national income. That is why Piketty says "the three most important concepts for analyzing the capitalist system are the capital/income ratio, the share of capital in income, and the rate of return on capital."[14] If there is a high ratio of national capital to national income, and a high return to capital, you are going to see a high distribution of a nation's income going to capital rather than labor. The micro implication is that companies will distribute more of their total revenue to stock owners as profits than to workers as wages. As the miners showed, and as the Occupy Wall Street movement shouted out, this is an inflammatory situation.

Piketty is doing something innovative by focusing us on the capital in capitalism. It's remarkable that today's economists have largely ignored the anatomy of wealth. Piketty wants us to know everything important about capital and wealth. What type of capital—land, machinery, financial assets, or private homes, for example—has the most value, and has it changed over the centuries? Is wealth mostly private, or public? Is it high or low relative to wages? Is it growing or diminishing as a share of the overall economy? What share of national income goes to the income derived from capital, and what share goes to the wages or salaries paid to labor? How much inequality of income and wealth exists? And why does it all matter?

Mainstream economists might find Piketty's questions innovative but politically charged and hinting of heresy. They might be secretly shame-faced about not having asked these "capital questions" about capital itself. But they might also say that market theories have already proved that there should be no great problem or injustice, since capital's return is justified by its productivity—and the split between the amount of income going to capital and labor is not likely to be either an economic or moral problem in the long term. Most professional economists believe that the market adjusts to ensure that this split is fair, reflecting the contribution or productivity of both capital and workers.

What would progressives or even radicals such as Marx think of Piketty's approach to thinking about wealth or capital? Marx would certainly agree that doing an anatomy of wealth or capital and looking at the share of income going to capital versus labor are crucially important. He would applaud Piketty resurrecting one of the great questions about capitalism and social justice: What is the right and fair way to distribute or split national income between capital and labor? And Piketty's findings, that the return to capital is high and that the share of national income going to capital (amount of dividends, interests, rent, and other returns to owners of wealth) rather than to labor (wages or salaries of workers) is still startlingly great, would confirm Marx's own prediction, although Marx thought that overproduction, declining profits, and extremely low wages would lead to the collapse of capitalism. Piketty's view is that capitalism may survive but the workers are going to get the short end of the stick; the capitalists are going to get the long end, the more their capital accumulates.

Four or five big findings in Parts 1 and 2 about wealth and capital stand out. First, the amount of wealth and the returns to capital in capitalist societies relative to income have remained high over the past three centuries. Before you say that doesn't surprise you, recall that most social thinkers predicted that the huge wealth of the landed nobility and richest dynastic families in feudalism and in early capitalism—which grew ever larger and dwarfed the paltry amount of income received by serfs and workers—would reverse under capitalism. As capitalism developed, the huge and clearly unjust wealth of the nobility would presumably diminish, as the education of the workers and their rising productivity led to rising wages and a changing split between income from capital and from labor, favoring the latter. Moreover, when there's a lot of capital, one extra unit produces little new wealth, meaning that the marginal productivity of capital declines as capital increases, suggesting a decline in capital as capitalism matures.

Piketty finds quite the contrary. The stock of wealth or capital has remained very high—in both absolute and relative terms. It has not declined in importance as education has increased and labor productivity has risen. Nor has it declined as capital has grown in size, and its marginal productivity declined. And the growth of technology has not reduced the size of capital relative to labor but seems to require at least the same, if not more. Capital is still the dominating factor in capitalism, as it was in earlier eras.

This is evident in the trillions of dollars owned by a relatively small number of capital holders and huge banks on Wall Street. They are the new aristocracy rising in the twenty-first century, and their wealth may well be unprecedented in human history.

Capital is overwhelmingly privately rather than publicly owned, the second of Piketty's key findings. Since the size of government has grown in developed nations such as the United States and in Europe, that might seem surprising. But waves of privatization both in the developed and developing world, and global policies encouraging selling off of public assets to companies or individuals, has led capital to be overwhelmingly private. This might surprise conservatives who think that the expansion of government has led to public ownership exceeding private ownership.

Third, and less surprising, the composition of capital has changed dramatically. Three hundred years ago, most wealth or capital consisted of agricultural land. Today, as agriculture is a much smaller fraction of the economy, capital has become largely divided, almost equally, between (1) corporate and financial assets, such as stocks and bonds, and (2) real estate and nonagricultural land, including commercial property, resources underground such as oil or minerals, and private homes.

Fourth, the capital/income ratio—the relation of the size of capital or wealth to the national income—has remained relatively stable over the past three hundred years. In Europe that ratio has hovered around 7 to 1 while in the United States it is significantly lower, about 4 to 1. The only exception is the long war period and beyond—covering about five decades in the mid-twentieth century—when capital in both Europe and the United States, but especially Europe, experienced "shocks" that led to destruction of much national wealth, of which we will say more in discussing inequality. Since the early 1970s, though, the capital/income ratio has reverted to the prewar period, and Piketty argues that we might see the ratio spike around the world in the twenty-first century, to the prewar period, around 6 or 7 to 1.

What does all this tell us? Most of all, that capital remains central to capitalism and that all the labor—skilled or not—in the world has not created rises in income that have diminished the relative size of wealth in the world. Because wealth ownership has always been extremely unequal—much more unequal than income—this means, as we see when we turn to the subject of inequality, that not only is concentrated wealth as big—or nearly as big—a factor in our world as in the medieval world or during the gilded capitalism of the nineteenth century, but that prospects for greater equality and the well-being of the majority of workers do not bode well.

To see the implications more clearly, imagine that the capital/income ratio rises to almost infinity, with wealth unimaginably huge while income has become tiny. What would such a society look like? One way that Piketty puts it is that the past would consume the present. Big holders of accumulated wealth (mainly the rich) would reign supreme for a very long time in the future over those who do not have wealth (the majority of workers), because the latter do not have a means of making enough income from work that would begin to change the situation. That sounds entirely contrary to the mainstream economist view that capitalism is a good system because it will overcome the huge inequalities of the past.

Piketty does not foresee the Marxist apocalypse of capitalist collapse, because he believes that Marx underestimated the growth of education and technology that would increase the productivity of workers and thus allow enough growth in wages or income to keep the capital/income ratio from getting too extreme. Nonetheless, his projection of 7 to 1 as a likely twenty-first-century ratio of wealth to income suggests something very different than what most Americans have come to believe about capitalism. The reigning wisdom is that capitalism moves us away from an aristocracy of wealth and allows most of the population an opportunity to move upward rather than being permanently disinherited. No! Piketty argues that the "deep structure" of capitalism has not changed, and capital in the twenty-first century will more than likely increase its size relative to wages and national income.[15] And what of the capital/labor split? Piketty argues that economists have traditionally assumed a "balanced growth" in capitalism—or a rise in human skills and thus wages created by education and high technology—that would lead to a higher split for labor in the future than in the past. But once again, Piketty argues they are dead wrong; there is absolutely no reason to believe that a better split for labor is in the cards. Capital in the twenty-first century could take even a bigger share, largely for political reasons. This allusion to political power is crucial (and the subject of the next section on inequality) because it is at the heart of the issue—and hints at where economics has gone off the rails and tells us little about the real economy.

Piketty does not deny, of course, the importance of technology and rise in skills. But he says that "progress toward economic and technological rationality need not imply progress toward democratic and meritocratic rationality. The primary reason for this is simple: technology, like the market, has neither limits nor morality."[16] Translation: the miners killed in South Africa as they protested for higher wages may be poster children for the twenty-first century. The next generation of miners and other disinherited folks will be like the American workers at McDonald's and Walmart—who, at this writing, are in a battle to raise their wages to a living wage of $15 an hour. They are in a life-and-death struggle to increase their wages and thus workers' share of national income. But there is absolutely no economic reason to believe that the workers will win, and serious political reasons to believe that they will lose, ensuring that a new century of workers might die fighting for their decent and fair share, perhaps for their very survival.

Part 3 is the *piece de resistance*. It is Piketty's analysis of inequality, and it is a shot heard round the world. He tells a sobering story: that capitalism, always deeply unequal, seems likely in the twenty-first century to get even more unequal. The 1% may soak up and pass on most new wealth created to their children, leaving a super-majority disinherited. Piketty is not saying this is inevitable, but he argues there is absolutely nothing in a perfectly functioning market system to prevent this from happening. This glum scenario is perhaps the most probable outcome if we do not politically mobilize to stop it.

Vast inequality of wealth is already a global phenomenon. The 1% in 2010 owned 50 percent of the world's wealth—and their children seem destined to inherit the world. The top 10 percent owned 80 to 90 percent.[17] You can do the arithmetic. The bottom 80 percent—the disinherited super-majority of the world—owned only 10 to 20 percent. And the numbers appear to be getting worse.

Inequality comes in two packages: inequalities of income, and inequalities of wealth. Wealth inequality is always much higher than income inequality, and it has more serious implications for democracy and for destroying the American Dream. But Piketty starts Part 3 looking at income inequality, because it is arguably the big story in the United States.

Income inequality itself comes in two packages: inequality of income from capital (dividends, interest, rent, etc.), and inequality of income from labor (wages and salaries). They are both moving in the wrong direction in the United States, but it is inequality in income from labor—the difference between low-income workers and high-income employees—that is rising and storming the nation like a hurricane.

At the center of this super-storm is the rising class of "super-managers," who are almost all high-level corporate executives. The exploding salary of this tip-top of the income hierarchy becomes more explosive the higher you go. Those making $200,000 a year are getting big raises, but those making $500,000 annually are getting even bigger raises, and those making more than $1 million are getting by far the biggest raises. The 1%, as the Occupy movement claimed, is taking much of the new income, but Occupy needed to zoom in on the very, very top; it is actually the top 0.1 percent of the 1% who are pulling down the real increases in money.[18]

It is the astonishing rate in the increase of the salaries of the already best-paid employees of the world that is the heart of the crisis. In most of the labor force, wages have stagnated for thirty years. But at the tip-top, particularly among executives on Wall Street, the dizzying growth in compensation is totally unprecedented! And this, says Piketty, is making the United States the most unequal nation in terms of income from labor of any nation in the history of the world.

Why, then, are the millionaire and multimillionaire top executives getting such huge raises each year when the majority's wages are flat? This is where Piketty's analysis becomes particularly interesting. Economists tend to argue that wages at all levels are determined by the productivity of the worker. Piketty asserts that this makes no sense at all in explaining tip-top salaries, showing instead that it is power rather than productivity that matters. Top managers can largely set their own salaries. Here, Piketty begins a crucial assault on mainstream economic theory and its legitimation of market rationality. As I flesh out in the fourteen capital questions discussed later in this book, he argues that the entire market theories of economists about productivity and wages ignore the political and social forces that shape wages and the labor market. To understand top executive pay "is obviously a question for sociology, psychology, cultural and political history, and the study of beliefs and perceptions at least as much as for economics per se."[19] The economists' theories are less science and more ideological justifications for paying the richest employees ever more at the expense of workers who are barely scraping by.

Turning to inequality of wealth, Piketty describes a very similar picture but with even more dangerous consequences for democracy and society. He shows a huge wealth gap that has increased rapidly since 1970, beginning to return to Old European or Gilded Age levels. The wealth gap has historically been much larger in Europe (reflecting the history of aristocracy in Old Europe), but the United States is beginning to catch up, with more and more wealth concentration in the top 1 percent since the 1970s. By 2010, the 10 percent wealthiest Americans' share of national wealth exceeded 70 percent and the 1%'s share was about 35 percent.[20] Piketty characterizes plausible scenarios about future wealth inequality in this way: "The conditions are ideal for an 'inheritance society' to prosper—where by 'inheritance society' I mean a society characterized by both a very high concentration of wealth and a significant persistence of large fortunes from generation to generation."[21] An "inheritance society," which he also calls "patrimonial capitalism," is the opposite of how Americans see their society, which they view as a capitalist "opportunity society," in which hard work and talent trump inheritance. It also contradicts mainstream economists' market theory that as capitalism develops it "lifts all boats." Piketty's historical data over three hundred years show that the economists' theory never held water, except in the unique, long mid-twentieth-century era. Capitalism has almost always been patrimonial, and, since the 1970s, we have seen a trend back to the "inheritance society" that has almost always defined capitalism.

But why? Is there an economic or other social theory that proves wealth will always tend to concentrate toward the 1%? Piketty says no: "I take this to be a historical fact, not a logical necessity."[22] There is no iron law of wealth concentration; for Piketty, it is contingent on many factors, most of all social and political forces and policies, as well as demographic factors, saving rates, and unpredictable "shocks" to capital or labor.

Piketty, who is disarmingly modest in his writing, explicitly rejects any notion that he is an economic Einstein, or that he has developed something equivalent to a new theory of relativity in physics. In fact, he, along with many of his critics, leans toward saying he offers no true theory of inequality; everything seems contingent and based on history and politics. But while this may be true, Piketty offers his own framework for analyzing inequality that has an Einsteinian feel. Piketty's $e = mc^2$ reads as follows: $r > g$.

As I noted earlier, r is the return on capital and g is the growth rate of the economy, equivalent to the growth of income. Piketty's fundamental law of inequality, if we can call it that, is that when $r > g$, inequality will increase. This is not rocket science. It says simply that if those holding capital—mostly the wealthiest people—are seeing a higher rate of return on their wealth than the rate of wage increases that most workers are experiencing, inequality will logically increase. This is less theory than mathematical tautology.

But the historical data are so strong that $r > g$ begins to feel like an iron law. "Throughout most of human history," Piketty observes, "the inescapable fact is that the rate of return on capital was always at least 10 to 20 times greater than the rate of growth of output (and income). Indeed this fact is to a large extent the very foundation of society itself."[23] Since 1700, the rate of return on capital (r) has hovered around 4.5–5 percent. During the same period, growth (g) has hovered between 1 and 2 percent. The only exception to this is the period of what Piketty repeatedly calls the "shocks to capital," in the several decades spanning the mid-twentieth century—when two world wars and the Great Depression combined with other factors to demolish much of accumulated wealth, and governmental policies encouraged education and high taxes on wealth and high income.

Economists have mistaken the equalizing trends in the twentieth century as a law of capitalism. But the larger historical perspective shows the opposite. That is why Piketty's historical research has begun to turn views of economics—and of markets—upside down.

The main factors increasing g—which Piketty calls forces of convergence—are the spread of education, the spread of knowledge, and the rise of more skilled labor. When combined with technology, these can increase productivity of workers and tend to push wages up. Population growth also can increase the growth rate, and all these factors contribute to more equality. Nonetheless, growth rates have historically been low—almost always below 1.5 percent or 2 percent—and a "low growth regime" is a recipe for inequality.

The forces of divergence—that increase inequality—have proved to be historically stronger. R has averaged around 4.5 percent to 5 percent and never over many centuries has been below 2 percent. Why has r stayed so high? Here, Piketty acknowledges, the history is stronger than theory. He mentions the savings rate, which is often significant as a hedge against future downturns or bad luck. When people—especially the wealthy—save even a small fraction of their income or wealth, the rate of increase of wealth—and thus r—will likely grow. Piketty also mentions policies that discourage investment in education and reduce spread of knowledge that is so important to increasing wages and growth, another factor increasing r relative to g. Political policies and social norms that favor the rich and corporations through taxation or trade can also increase return on capital.

From the beginning, wealth has been historically highly concentrated—with the majority having almost no wealth. Piketty says that

people with inherited wealth need save only a portion of their income from capital to see that capital grow more quickly than the economy as a whole. Under such conditions, it is almost inevitable that inherited wealth will dominate wealth amassed from a lifetime's labor by a wide margin, and the concentration of capital attain extremely high levels—levels potentially incompatible with the meritocratic values and principles of social justice fundamental to modern democratic societies.[24]

This leads Piketty to forecast the probable return of inherited wealth as a dominant force, much as it was in the age of Balzac and Austen. He shows first that inherited wealth is already in the United States at least 50 to 60 percent of total US capital or wealth, with some arguing more like 70 to 80 percent, similar to that in Europe.[25] He also shows that the "inheritance flow," the annual economic flow of inheritances and gifts as a percentage of national income, is now rapidly surpassing the savings rate and is nearly 15 percent of annual income, and could easily rise in the twenty-first century to 25 percent, as it was in the Gilded Age a century or more ago.[26]

The rise of inheritance grows with the concentration of wealth in large fortunes, such as those being amassed by corporate executives to-day. Huge corporate compensation packages for CEOs assures that great wealth will be passed on to their children, turning them into a "rentier" or inheritance class that need never work a day in their lives, much like the gentry in Balzac and Austen's era, who saw work as degrading, and proper only for the mass of workers. As fortunes grow larger, inheritance becomes even a bigger factor, because the larger the fortune, the higher the return on capital. This is because larger capital hires better money managers and lawyers, or finds better ways to evade taxes. Piketty compares the high return on the huge multibillion-dollar endowments of Harvard with the very modest returns on the small endowments of the average school, illustrating that as fortunes grow, so do the returns on capital, leading to ever larger inheritances passed down from generation to generation, whether of an institution or a family.

The consequences are devastating—for opportunity, mobility, and democracy. If we are returning to the age of Balzac and Austen, the idea of the American Dream will become pure myth. Mobility will fall, as it declines when inequality increases. Moreover, even for those who work hard and rise as far as possible, they will never live a life of more than the most modest means, with no chance of living the life of those with inherited wealth. Democracy is in the greatest jeopardy, as money is power, and inherited fortunes are power on steroids.

In his final section, Piketty turns to solutions. He has shown that twenty-first-century capitalism is very likely destined to return to Gilded Age rates of extreme inequality that threaten democracy, undermine social justice, and can create another economic collapse. This is not inevitable, but markets, even when working perfectly, do not in any way deter or prevent this looming crisis. The only way to change course is through strong political interventions, which Piketty fleshes out in the final section of his book.

Piketty's solutions revolve around spreading wealth and limiting the rise of dynastic fortunes. His goal is not the Marxist one of replacing capitalism with socialism, but creating enough equality to ensure everyone the equal rights specified in the 1948 UN Declaration of Human Rights: rights to food, shelter, freedom from poverty, health care, good education, and a job paying a living wage.

Piketty seeks a "social state" rather than socialism. The contrast with Marx is obvious, but the solutions themselves are not entirely different. Both Piketty and Marx see an unacceptable concentration of wealth and power in the capitalist class. And both seek a solution through spreading the ownership of capital more widely, to preserve democracy, create a just distribution of wealth, fund the state's provisioning of social rights to the people, and protect the inalienable rights of the entire population.

How does one achieve this? In his book, Piketty focuses primarily on taxation. It is obvious that taxes play an important role in the distribution of wealth and income. Piketty lays out an ambitious set of progressive policies to tax both income and wealth, but he recognizes that taxes are not the only tool in his kit. While he does not discuss them in detail, he is a supporter of expansive social services for health, retirement, and education, as well as regulation of financial markets, worker ownership, and a wide range of other policies that are generally part of the European welfare state and can help spread wealth and curb excessive inequality.

Why does he focus, then, on taxes? This flows from an important philosophical and historical perspective. Piketty writes, "Taxation is not a technical matter. It is pre-eminently a political and philosophical issue, perhaps the most important of all political issues. Without taxes society has no common destiny, and collective action is impossible. This has always been true. At the heart of every major political upheaval lies a fiscal revolution."[27] Americans, of all people, he says, should recognize this, since the American Revolution "was born when subjects of the British colonies decided to take their destiny in hand and set their own taxes. (No taxation without representation.)"[28]

1

♦ ♦ ♦

THE PIKETTY PHENOMENON

What explains the "Piketty phenomenon"—the unprecedented best-selling success of a scholarly tome filled with numbers about the economies of Europe and the United States? Will it be a book like The Feminine Mystique *by Betty Friedan or* Silent Spring *by Rachel Carson or* The Other America *by Michael Harrington that creates a new consciousness and politics in the United States? What are the conditions and forces that may make this possible? And who are the two Pikettys, the two different voices of Thomas Piketty, who are likely to fuel major debates about the meaning of the book, and keep the social conversation about it exciting and provocative?*

In late spring 2014, a nearly seven-hundred-page scholarly book by a French professor of economics, filled with data and charts, did something extraordinary. Even before its official publication date, it shot up on the best-sellers list of the *New York Times* and up to the top of Amazon, perching at number one for many weeks after publication. It sold out its first printing by the Belknap Press of Harvard University in the first month, and remained a best seller as Harvard rushed to get tens of thousands of new books printed. While this all started in the United States, it quickly spread around the world, with books selling like hotcakes in almost every country. The world's most famous intellectuals and pundits flooded the newspaper columns and Internet with commentary about the book. Many argued it was one of the defining books of the new century, destined to help shape public discourse for decades to come.

The French professor is named Thomas Piketty, and his book is called *Capital in the Twenty-First Century*. Piketty became instantly one of the most famous thinkers and writers in the world. The book became one of the most widely discussed books on the planet. In a world where almost everything has a very short shelf life, Piketty's book kept selling and kept provoking more conversation, more reviews, more conferences, more follow-up questions and scholarship, more book club attention, and more controversy.

Thus was born "the Piketty phenomenon." What is it all about, and does it have lasting importance?

The global reception of the book, the astonishing range of luminaries who have endorsed it, the widely expressed view of the book as seminal—all raise an intriguing possibility. The book might be one of those rare works that transforms the national conversation. This is possible in scores of countries, where the book became a best seller, but especially in the United States, the developed country that might be the most transformed if the arguments of the new book came to be widely discussed.

Of course, it is possible that the book and the sensation that followed might be eventually seen as a flash in the pan. In the flood of commentary right after the book's publication, many scholars saw flaws in the data, limits in the theory, and problems with the framing of the most basic concepts. Some saw it as flat wrong, full of contradictions, or an ideological polemic masked in oceans of data. In a dismissive, highly negative review, the prominent progressive economist James Galbraith described much of the conceptualization and analysis as flawed, and the policy proposals even worse:

> Piketty's further policy views come in two chapters to which the reader is bound to arrive, after almost five hundred pages, a bit worn out. These reveal him to be neither radical nor neoliberal, nor even distinctively European. Despite having made some disparaging remarks early on about the savagery of the United States, it turns out that Thomas Piketty is a garden-variety social welfare democrat in the mold, largely, of the American New Deal.[1]

Others, in contrast, argued that the book started an intellectual revolution. It challenged existing intellectual schools; created a fundamentally new way of thinking about economy, politics, and society; and brought together more rigorous data than any prior work of scholarship on some of the most important issues in the present century. Nobel economist

Paul Krugman wrote, "Piketty has transformed our economic discourse; we'll never talk about wealth and inequality the same way we used to." Krugman says as well, "This is a book that will change both the way we think about society and the way we do economics."[2]

Part of the very diverse reactions reflect what I will call the existence of the "two Pikettys." Like many brilliant thinkers, Piketty is not of a single mind. He sometimes approaches his subject almost as two different thinkers. The two Pikettys are my way of interpreting two different currents of thinking that Piketty has set in motion. Piketty 1 is a Keynesian economist who in this book focuses on abstract economic aggregates or statistical groupings as well as economic forces that appear to be detached from real people and politics. His subject seems to be limited to inequality, his methods are historical and descriptive but otherwise relatively conventional in Keynesian economics, and while he introduces exciting new ideas, his solutions seem to be relatively narrow. Piketty 1 embraces capitalism and is trying to save it from itself.

Piketty 2 is a humanistic social, political, and economic free thinker who is concerned with basic human rights and social justice. Piketty 2 has serious concerns about capitalism as a system, its internal contradictions, and its social injustice. He sometimes uses mechanistic economic arguments and statistical groupings, but he rejects much of conventional economics as narrow and pseudoscience. His concern is the dignity of real people and the fairness of an economic order that is shaped not just by economic forces but unequal political power. Piketty 2 is interested in policy prescriptions, like Piketty 1, but he is also interested in fiery protests and social movements, such as Occupy Wall Street, where citizens try to change the direction of history.

The huge response to the book is partly a response to the just-under-the-surface conversation between Piketty 1 and Piketty 2. Some commentators focus on the ideas reflecting Piketty 1, and others see Piketty 2. The Piketty legacy will be a conversation about a new set of vital issues—some highlighted by Piketty 1 and some by Piketty 2—about capitalism, equality, and justice in the twenty-first century.

The existence of the two Pikettys is a sign of strength. The renowned sociologist Alvin Gouldner wrote a brilliant book, *The Two Marxisms*, distinguishing between "scientific Marxism" and "critical Marxism," both representing authentic legacies of Marx but reflecting different sides of his thinking.[3] The two Marxisms reflect more the way two different groups of thinkers after Marx interpreted him, rather than two completely different voices of Marx. But the two Marxisms—and now the two Pikettys—contribute to a much bigger and more interesting conversation. Eventually the two Marxisms led to two quite different traditions, one represented by Stalinist regimes and the other by Social Democratic regimes.

The same could be true of the two Pikettys. This book partly illuminates the two different threads of conversation that might flow from Piketty's book and the conflict that could emerge between Piketty 1 and Piketty 2 political movements. The two Pikettys will help clarify Piketty himself, but I am more interested here in looking beyond Piketty at the new conversation that has already begun.

The initial fireworks about Piketty's book—and about Piketty (or both Pikettys)—inevitably will die down and, at this writing, have already begun to do so. But while the book has serious limitations, it has the *potential* to be a game changer, in two ways. It has enough intellectual originality and firepower that it can help breed a new way of thinking in the university, the mass media, and the larger culture. It also has the potential to fire up a new political wave of change helping catalyze new social movements for change, much as Betty Friedan's book *The Feminine Mystique* helped created a new feminist movement, Michael Harrington's book *The Other America* helped give rise to Lyndon Johnson's War on Poverty, and Rachel Carson's book *Silent Spring* helped give birth to modern environmentalism.[4]

Even if the book itself were to fade—a real possibility in a world with a very short attention span—the ideas and methods it has brought to light are likely to live on. A new conversation has already started among the intelligentsia. It is blending with new forces in mass media, politics, and religion; a month after Piketty's book was published, the world was dubbing the new pope the "Piketty Pope," after he tweeted that "inequality is the root of social evil."[5] It is also likely that it will help catalyze already existing—and new—social movements for equality and justice, successors to the Occupy movement that will press for change, even if younger generations do not remember Piketty or his book.

The questions that the book has now put on the table are not easily stuffed back in the drawer. This is not only because of the power and originality of the book but also due to its uncanny resonance with the era in which it emerged. Since the 2007–2008 financial meltdown, questions about the stability and justice of capitalism have rippled across the country—and the world. As the Wall Street bankers who drove the nation into the ditch got bailed out, too many ordinary Americans lost their jobs, their houses, or their pensions. The contrast in the fate of the people on top and the rest of us is too large and painful to ignore.

Moreover, the bailouts of the rich and abandonment of workers began to make clear a curious contradiction. We seem to be creating a socialism for the rich, where the government protects them when they fail. But it's "you're on your own"—the free market—for the working people and the poor. The government is not going to protect or save them.

This is not the way capitalism is supposed to work. And ordinary Americans—who are bearing the brunt of the pain—had begun to realize this several years before Piketty's book appeared. The rippling concern was evident in polls showing anger toward big corporations, in the popularity of films like *The Wolf of Wall Street,* in growing pitchfork populism on both the Right and Left against a corporate government ignoring the people, in the amount of books and protests about inequality, in the politics of Occupy Wall Street and new movements to raise the minimum wage by fast-food and Walmart workers.

As a troubled, weak economy lingered after the Great Recession, the public increasingly had new questions and wanted new solutions. The continuing and deep crises in the economy and what appeared to be a rigged political system raised with new intensity issues about the basic equality and social justice of capitalism and our nation. It just so happened that these questions coincided almost perfectly with the questions raised in Piketty's book:

- Is extreme inequality built into the DNA of capitalism?
- Is America the cradle of opportunity?
- Are we the world's famed class-free society?
- Is there any limit to the growing gap between the very, very wealthy and everyone else?
- Does wealth trickle down from the top?
- Is the American Dream still alive?
- Is hard work rewarded by the system?
- Is the market a meritocracy?
- Is capitalism consistent with democracy?

- Is there any realistic solution to extreme inequality?
- Is there any serious alternative to capitalism?

What Piketty did was show that these questions can no longer be dismissed as anti-American or extremist rhetoric. He put too many disturbing numbers on the table, not only in his book but up on the Web for all to see. But Piketty did more. He offered ways of thinking about the growing number of questions that both intellectuals and ordinary Americans had not heard before. And while Piketty was modest, and claimed not to offer definitive answers, he offered just enough possible answers to excite thoughtful people—and pull them deeper into a new conversation.

When an author's subject and approach dovetails perfectly with the problems of the era, and is written in a simple, disarming, and original fashion that points to new solutions, a landmark book can emerge. It will not be a definitive blueprint, but it can help catalyze and focus a new conversation that had already begun. This is what explains the "Piketty phenomenon": his book began to crystallize a set of deep public concerns that had already been emerging——about inequality, class conflict, the 1%, dynastic families and inherited wealth, meritocracy, mobility, and social justice—and helped to channel them into a new national conversation. Piketty did not provide all the answers, by any means, but he provided data that could help put the conversation on a serious empirical foundation, and he set the table with questions, like those above, that inevitably will galvanize a large part of the nation in years to come.

I have organized this book around fourteen key questions; there are more I could have chosen. These questions constitute the curriculum of a new public American discourse in the twenty-first century. A wide discussion of these questions could have a revolutionary impact—and may transform both the university and the political system, ultimately changing the nation and the world.

Discussion Questions

1. Have you read Piketty?
2. Do you think Piketty's book will be a game changer?
3. Has it already changed the American conversation about inequality, capitalism, and the 1%?

4. Do you understand the different views of the two Pikettys?
5. Are Americans more likely to respond to Piketty 1, or Piketty 2?
6. What groups will champion the new conversation we need after Piketty's book?
7. What groups will try to stop that conversation dead in its tracks?

2

♦ ♦ ♦

WHAT'S THE MATTER
WITH ECONOMICS?

Is American economics useful for understanding the American economy—or has it helped contribute to a false construction of how capitalism and economies actually work? What has gone wrong with the economics profession, as it has divorced itself from the study of history, social mores, and political power? Are there more useful ways to study economics? Can sociology, history, and political science help start a new way of studying the economy? What about reviving the grand tradition of political economy that helped launch the social sciences and focused on capitalism and its alternatives?

Thomas Piketty, a French economist, fled America and returned to his native Paris after a few years in the United States, where he taught in the economics department at the Massachusetts Institute of Technology. He was highly respected as a mathematical economist. But he left the United States because he felt that the deeper he got into his equations and the American way of doing economics, the less he understood about the US and world economy. Describing the success of his mathematical dissertation at MIT, he says, "Something strange happened: I was only too aware of the fact that I knew nothing at all about the world's economic problems."[1] He goes on to comment about professional economists, many of whom are his friends, that "they must set aside their contempt for other disciplines and their absurd claim to greater scientific legitimacy, despite the fact that they know almost nothing about anything."[2]

Piketty tells this personal story at the beginning of his book, and it is very important, although often overlooked. His indictment of American economics is partial and respectful, but white hot. He notes that "very clever" American economists—almost drunk with their mathematical equations and models—view themselves as the only true social "scientists," and says, hilariously, that some reputedly put on white lab coats at their university departments to broadcast their stature as men and women of science.

Despite this, Piketty 1 sees great value in scientific rigor—and in economic science. So does Piketty 2, but Piketty 2 sees in American economics as much pseudoscience as science. He writes,

> To put it bluntly the discipline of economics has yet to get over its childish passion for mathematics and for purely theoretical and often highly ideological speculation, at the expense of historical research and collaboration with the other social sciences. Economists are all too often preoccupied with petty mathematical problems of interest only to themselves. This obsession with mathematics is an easy way of acquiring the appearance of scientificity without having to answer the far more complex questions posed by the world we live in.[3]

Anyone who has looked at his book knows that Piketty (both 1 and 2) is a passionate "numbers guy" who believes in data and evidence. There are numbers and charts on hundreds of pages, and the credibility of his work undoubtedly rests on the unprecedented amount of data he has collected. So Piketty's complaint is hardly against rigorous empirical research, at which he is a master by virtually everyone's account, but the pretensions of economics as a science and the gaping failure of American economics to move from clean and elegant mathematical equations on the blackboard to the messy, muddy realities of the real world.

But Piketty argues that the problem is deeper. As professionalism began to take root in American universities in the late nineteenth century, economists happily segregated their discipline from all others, viewing the economy as a *deus ex machina* operating by universal laws abstracted from the rest of the humanities and social fields. The great earlier thinkers about society and economy—from Adam Smith to David Ricardo to Karl Marx—saw the economy as embedded in history, politics, culture, and society itself.[4] The new twentieth-century US professional economist, though, saw no reason to dip into history, culture, or sociology. The economy had a life of its own, its most important laws as independent of society as those of physics. It was this beautiful universalism—the ability to abstract away from the varieties of social experience and discover transcendent laws—that made economics the "queen of the social sciences."

Both of the two Pikettys are skeptical of this arrogance of professional economists, especially in the United States. Piketty 1, though, relies heavily on abstract and mechanistic economic theory, despite his cautions about it. Piketty 2, the voice of humanism and democracy, has some of the same contradictions. He sees virtue in the mechanics of economic systems that economists study, but he wants to move beyond abstract economic forces to social, political, and cultural arguments—although he, too, seems trapped in his economistic training. He, though, views economics as too important to be left to professional economists or even to sociologists and political scientists; it is a subject for every citizen. He views the professional, specialized academic approach as the death of any serious possibility of understanding the economy and the real world.

Piketty 2, and to some degree Piketty 1, argues that economics is not physics, and, more profoundly, *economics itself is not just economics*. Economic laws and market rules and outcomes reflect not only abstract laws of supply and demand—or factors intrinsic to purely economic arrangements (which Piketty 2 hints can never exist)—but social mores, cultural values, and political power. In different societies, with different histories and power elites, market economies—or any other type of economy—will operate by different rules with different outcomes.

Piketty argues that to understand economies, we need to reconstruct the study of economics. The new discipline he suggests we need is "political economy," which, of course, is not new at all but a resurrection of the tradition of the preprofessional great theorists of the eighteenth and nineteenth centuries, such as Adam Smith and Karl Marx. Political economy blends the study of politics with the study of economy, as they are inseparable (see my own book with Yale Magrass, which is an "invitation to political economy" that expands on Piketty's own deeply critical view of professional economics).[5] Piketty 2 hints that political power shadows and shapes everything happening in the economy. But even that is too narrow an interpretation, since he argues that in addition to politics, we must study history, culture, and sociology to get a grasp of how economies operate.[6]

Piketty is hardly the first to make some of these critiques of American economics. Paul Krugman, an American Nobel laureate in economics, has denounced American "blackboard economics," by which he means the almost childlike obsession with mathematical prowess and technical wizardry that both he and Piketty view as sophomoric and dangerous, removing the study of economics from the study of real economies.[7] Robert Kuttner, one of our most astute economic thinkers and writers, wrote more than twenty-five years ago that in their secret heart of hearts, economists are terrified that they would have to come out of the closet and admit that they are sociologists, since the economy is really just part of the larger society and is shaped by its values and power elites.[8]

Piketty tells us he could never have written his book had he stayed in America and its economics profession. But he should have acknowledged more. Piketty has been deeply shaped by American economics. The most serious limitations of his work, reflecting the louder voice of Piketty 1 in this book, involve his failure to more fully move beyond the economics that he critiques. He fails to integrate enough of the sociological and political ideas that he acknowledges lie at the center of any true understanding of the economy. Nonetheless, his commitment—which is really the voice of Piketty 2—to moving beyond economics to study the economy is unambiguous. He writes,

> The truth is that economics should never have sought to divorce itself from the other social sciences and can advance only in conjunction with them. The social sciences collectively know too little to waste time on foolish disciplinary squabbles. If we are to progress in our understanding of the historical dynamics of the wealth distribution and the structure of social classes, we must obviously take a pragmatic approach and avail ourselves of the methods of historians, sociologists, and political scientists. . . . We must start with fundamental questions and try to answer them. Disciplinary disputes and turf wars are of little or no importance. In my mind, this is as much a work of history as of economics.[9]

Later, he goes further, saying that we need to resurrect a political economy in the spirit of Smith and Marx, and that "economics" is necessarily as much sociology, culture, and politics as of history and politics and economics itself.[10]

We need a new conversation about how to reconstruct academic disciplines and university departments. Piketty has given that conversation a boost. But in his own work, he does not go nearly far enough in integrating social and political analysis into his own thinking. This failure makes clear how we need to move the conversation beyond Piketty: toward an intense focus on political power, state policy, and social movements as major shapers of inequality as well as of markets and capitalism itself.[11]

Discussion Questions

1. What kind of university would have kept Piketty in the United States and allowed him to write the book about the big ideas that he has?
2. Should we reorganize departments—and make them all interdisciplinary around big questions—like inequality, war and peace, capitalism, and climate change?
3. How can we revive the tradition of political economy in which Piketty sees himself working?
4. Should we have an Interdisciplinary Program on Capitalist Studies? A Department of Economic History? An Interdisciplinary Program of Critical Thinking? More departments of Political Economy?
5. Is American economics still viable in the wake of Piketty's critique, and how does it need to change?
6. Can sociology, political science, history, and literature begin to take on the big questions of political economy and capitalism in the spirit that Piketty proposes?

3

♦ ♦ ♦

ECONOMICS WITH CLASS

What is class as Piketty sees it? What are the main myths about class in America that Piketty's work begins to explode? Has Piketty started or changed the conversation about class in America? What are the political implications?

America has long prided itself on being the society without a divisive social class system. Many Americans say there is no class system at all in America. Class was a European phenomenon, and American exceptionalism was built on creating a society free of the ancient and deep inequalities of Old Europe. The American founders, especially Thomas Jefferson, highlighted this egalitarian vision in the Declaration of Independence, which was really a declaration of independence from European class-based and caste-based societies, that forever separated the aristocracy and wealthy merchants from the commoners, workers, and serfs. Jefferson highlighted that America was founded as a historically new experiment, committed first and foremost to everyone's equal rights to life, liberty, and the pursuit of happiness. America meant the right of everyone to succeed, to have equal opportunity if not equal results, and be happy without suffering the indignities of extreme or unbridgeable economic divisions.

By almost any definition of class, this meant that America rejected a class system built around deep and permanent inequalities. Economic differences among Americans—to be consistent with the founders' lofty rhetoric and ideals—had to be very different than the traditional concept of relatively fixed and impermeable classes developed in Old Europe.

The most rigid and fixed social differences are caste distinctions, which defined the feudal system of the European medieval era. The feudal caste society was the antithesis of what American founders claimed America would be. America would repudiate castes that defined people as different by "blood" or "essence." Caste differences are based on birth and cannot be changed, a view of inherently unequal people that Americans viewed as anathema to their new nation. Such profound inequality of humanity existed in slavery and gender relations, but the American promise, voiced by Jefferson in the Declaration of Independence, was that America would eventually transcend those differences, becoming the first great society free of castes. One of Piketty's most important contributions is to show how America never lived up to those ideas—and in the twenty-first century appears to be moving back to a version of the caste order of Old Europe.

Jefferson never claimed quite the same American exceptionalism about class as caste. He wanted to reduce class differences, and he imagined an America more egalitarian than eighteenth-century and early nineteenth-century Europe. American classes would have to be fluid, porous, and permeable to be consistent with Jefferson's ideals. The gap between one class and another could not be so great as to prevent people or their children from moving through hard work from one class to another. Jefferson did not imply that the American experiment required anything like perfect equality but that it would move closer than any prior society toward a meritocratic society where inequality would be limited and based on worth and hard work rather than birth.

Piketty shows that America never resembled or lived up to anything close to this Jeffersonian founding ideal. The ideal was always contradicted—in terrible ways—by dehumanizing caste differences of race and gender. Wealthy white men—northern merchants and southern planters—wrote the Constitution, seeking to maintain their property rights, and disenfranchising women and enslaving African Americans as lower castes. Even if we focus only on white men, America has been extremely unequal in the distribution of income and wealth from the very beginning, a view that Piketty's data confirm.

Piketty undermines the nation's long view of itself as a society free of harsh class divisions while discrediting also the idea that caste would disappear in capitalist America. And Piketty shows that America has now become more like Old Europe—a society permanently divided between a tiny 1% class of dynastic wealth and a disinherited class of struggling workers—than is New Europe. We are a society organized around the intertwined inequalities of class and caste.

To understand the class issue clearly, we need more clarity about the relation between inequality and class—and about the idea of class itself (in chapters to come we will explore the new idea of "caste classes" that I have drawn out of Piketty's work). Piketty's definition of class is close to that of the popular understanding of the term in the United States, which makes class and inequality difficult to distinguish. For most Americans, classes are simply groups sharing similar income or wealth. Classes come into being with inequality—they wouldn't exist in a perfectly equal society—and are a way of talking about it. The upper classes are made up of people with great wealth (the rich or capitalist classes), others of people in the middle range of income or wealth (the middle classes), and yet others of working or poor people (the lower classes) at the bottom of income and wealth hierarchies.

Piketty has embraced with slightly different language this conventional or colloquial concept of class. This proves to have advantages in resonating with the public but also disadvantages in building a robust theory and politics of class. For Piketty, and this is true especially of Piketty 1, class is simply a categorization distinguishing groups with different amounts of income and wealth. Piketty 2 offers a more socially and politically grounded view of class, but it gets less space in the book.[1]

Piketty is clear that his definition of class "is based entirely on statistical concepts such as deciles (top 10 percent, middle 40 percent, lower 50 percent, etc.) which are defined in exactly the same ways in different societies."[2] This is the voice of Piketty 1, who says that this approach "allows me to make rigorous and objective comparisons across time and space."[3] Piketty also says that this approach to class is based on the reality that "there is never a continuous break between social classes or between 'people' and the 'elite.'" He makes clear that class, for him, is a precise and accurate statistical way of capturing the way income or wealth is distributed: "The truth is that any representation of inequality that relies on a small number of categories is doomed to be crudely schematic, since the underlying social reality is always a continuous distribution."[4]

As we flesh out in the next chapter, this approach is notably different from Marx's idea of two great classes in capitalism: the "capitalist class" and the "working class." And while this leads to major differences in the class analysis of Piketty and Marx, which are indeed very important, the differences can be overstated. If we listen to the voice of Piketty 2, we find great appreciation of the Occupy movement's own conception of two great classes—the 1% and the 99%. Piketty 2 says, "To return for a moment to the Occupy Wall Street movement, what it shows is that the use of a common terminology, and in particular of the 'top centile'"—the 1%—can "be helpful in revealing the spectacular growth of inequality and may therefore serve as a useful tool for social interpretation and criticism. Even mass social movements can avail themselves of such a tool to develop unusual mobilizing themes such as 'We are the 99%.'"[5]

The hidden debate between Piketty 1 and 2 is reflected in his definition and use of class. Piketty shifts back and forth between the class dichotomy of the 1% and the 99%, which has strong political meaning and uses important to Piketty 2, and the multiple percentile classes that are the main focus of Piketty 1 and reflect his more abstracted statistical concept of class, representing the "continuous distribution" of income and wealth. His statistical classes are less politically illuminating, but, counterintuitively, Piketty ultimately uses them to resonate with the public and with social movements. This is because of his overwhelming focus on the 1%, which is the "percentile class" at the heart of his book. Ever since Occupy, the 1% and the 99% have become the most common and politically potent way to talk about class in America. This suggests that even those favoring more familiar class concepts of "owners" versus "workers" —and that includes myself, as I have long used a definition of class based on one's social position in production, that is, whether one is an owner or a worker—should not dismiss out of hand Piketty's percentile class approach.[6] It has important limitations, but it may bring Americans in an unexpected way back into a meaningful and political class conversation.

Even when not focused on the 1%, Piketty's percentile classes seem to be a lucid way of connecting inequality and class, and therefore making the idea of class more acceptable to an American public now keenly and often painfully aware of inequality itself. Piketty's work is full of discussion of quartiles, deciles, and centiles, dry and statistical terms. But they are intuitively understandable as groups perched at different positions of the income and wealth hierarchies. To be clear about the terminology, the top centile class is the richest 1% of Americans; the top decile class is the richest 10 percent; the top quartile class is the richest

25 percent; the bottom quartile class is the poorest 25 percent, and so on. Piketty focuses on the top centile (the 1%), which he calls the "dominant class"; the top decile (the upper 10 percent), which he calls the "upper class"; and the next 40 percent below the top decile, which he calls the "middle class," much less rich than the upper class but with some wealth, mainly in their homes. Below them are what he calls the "lower class," the bottom 50 percent or two quartiles, who have virtually no wealth at all.[7]

Piketty's "percentile classes" are thus simply ways of describing the statistical hierarchies of income and wealth; they are the numerical faces of inequality. Because inequality is a readily understood idea, most of the public can accept the classes that Piketty describes, which are simply steps on the inequality ladder. It doesn't require theoretical sophistication or a particular political persuasion to accept the reality of classes in Piketty's definition, and he acknowledges that he chose the lower, middle, and upper classes he names partly because they "correspond more closely to common usage."[8] By highlighting the extreme differences of people at different rungs in the hierarchy, Piketty's inequality data make crystal clear how drastically different the life situations of different American classes have become.

Piketty's analysis makes clear that the class where the action is today—and where an astonishing amount of income and wealth are concentrated—is, yes, the 1% branded by Occupy. He—and this is Piketty 2—implicitly lauds the movement: "The Occupy Wall Street movement aimed its criticism at the richest 1 percent," which Piketty notes is not only extremely rich but "is a large enough group to exert a significant influence on both the social landscape and the political and economic order."[9] Piketty also discusses the importance of the spectrum of wealth within each percentile class, including the 1% itself, showing that the top 1 percent of the 1%, made up of a tiny number of Wall Street and other corporate executives and dynastic, super-rich families, are worth many billions of dollars each and are scooping up most of the new income and wealth being created in America.[10] Piketty argues that we need to put under the microscope the 1% of capitalist aristocrats if we are to understand the twenty-first century.

Piketty proves the existence of America's enduring and deep class divide with encyclopedic data about the distribution of income and wealth over two to three centuries in America and Europe. The data are purely descriptive, but they are a conversational game changer. They change our understanding of ourselves and threaten American national identity and pride. His data lead inexorably to the conclusion that America has always been a class-driven society and has now become the most class-divided among the developed nations.[11]

Piketty has shown that we need to take a very skeptical view of our long national self-definition of equality and economic exceptionalism. We have not broken the mold of European class polarization; we have long been a highly unequal class society. We now are building a more rigid and extreme class society than the Europeans themselves. We are not—and never have been—a society that can define itself as being relatively class free. And it is irrational that we are a society that makes it difficult to talk about the very existence of class without seeming like an extremist. Piketty has shown the extreme or irrational view is to deny the existence of deep class divisions in America.

Piketty has opened up the possibility of a new mainstream conversation about inequality and class. Through most of American history, only fringe people, mainly on the Left, could or would use the language of class and describe the nation in the grips of a class crisis. No longer. Piketty has proved it is the elephant in the room, something the mainstream has to stop denying.

Piketty has shown that class denial is as delusional and dangerous as climate change denial. Of course, we know from the climate issue that that this does not ensure that mainstream America will talk and act decisively on the crisis. But it makes action more likely.

Discussion Questions

1. How do we revive a conversation about class in America?
2. How do we overcome class denial? Is it similar to overcoming climate change denial?
3. Will Piketty's book make it much easier to overcome class denial?
4. Are the 1% and the 99% fixtures in American conversation now?
5. Does Piketty put too little attention on the bottom 99%—and the classes they represent—by focusing so much on the top 1%?
6. Will mass media, professors, and politicians in America begin explicitly talking about class—with the focus on the new urban capitalist aristocracy that Piketty highlights?

4

♦ ♦ ♦

TRUE CLASS

What are the limits of Piketty's definition of class, and how do others entering the conversation define class? How do American liberals and progressives, European or American Social Democrats, or neo-Marxists—who work most closely in the intellectual tradition that gave rise to ideas about class—define class, and is their view consistent or inconsistent, better or worse, than Piketty's definitions and concepts? Has Piketty truly moved beyond the limits of professional economics that he critiques? How is the conversation about class likely to develop, and do we need to move beyond Piketty's own vision?

While Piketty has exploded the myth of a relatively class-free America, his work is better at describing the facts of inequality than explaining what class really means. Piketty 1 has started the conversation, but others will have to hear the more socially and politically grounded voice of Piketty 2, pick it up, and take it to the next level.

There are at least three interrelated problems with the Piketty 1 discussion. One is in the very definition of class, a problem that leads some to question whether class actually exists in the Piketty 1 world. The second is the failure to root class in the social world, since Piketty 1 does not discuss the history, institutions, culture, or consciousness of classes. Third, there is no explicit discussion of "class interests" and whether those interests, if they exist, pit classes in conflict with one another, leaving in question whether the existence of Piketty 1 classes implies the broad social struggles for power and justice that the concept of class has traditionally evoked.

Consider the definitional problem. As indicated above, Piketty 1 defines classes as statistical groupings perched at different steps of a continuous hierarchical distribution of unequal income or wealth. There can be an endless number of classes, the 1 percent wealthiest or top centile class, the 10 percent wealthiest or top decile class, the 25 percent richest or top quartile class, the poorest 10 percent or bottom decile class, the 1 percent poorest or the lowest centile class. And there are theoretically endless more—for example, the top 1 percent of the top centile class, the top 2 percent of the top centile class, and so on. This reflects the truth, writes Piketty, that "there is never a continuous break between social classes or between 'people' and the 'elite.'"[1] Whether any grouping can be singled out for study mainly depends on the theoretical or political concerns of those doing the naming.

As noted earlier, Piketty does name "for illustrative purposes" a few broad classes in the United States, such as the "dominant" 1%, the upper 10 percent, and the bottom 50 percent, which are useful in describing the hierarchies of income and wealth. But Piketty acknowledges that these are all still arbitrary ways of dividing up the class picture, and he could just as accurately have divided the society into 4 or 123 or 317 classes.[2]

While Marxists will reject this concept of class, for reasons discussed below, Piketty's "percentile" definitions have some theoretical merit. Income and wealth are, in fact, continuously distributed, and there is no perfectly "objective" way of deciding where to draw the line that defines different classes. The intention of the theorist always shapes the definition of class, as does the consciousness of the social groupings and their overall role in society, which varies historically and is quite different in different societies.

Nonetheless, Piketty 1, perhaps prodded by Piketty 2, acknowledges some of the problems of his definition of class. "The concepts of deciles and centiles," he notes, "are rather abstract and undoubtedly lack a certain poetry. It is easier for most people to identity with groups with which they are familiar: peasants or nobles, proletarians or bourgeois, office workers or top managers, waiters or traders. But the beauty of deciles and centiles is precisely that they enable us to compare inequalities that would otherwise be incomparable, using a common language that should in principle be acceptable to everyone."[3]

Well, not exactly. Conceptualizing classes as statistical aggregates such as deciles or centiles reflects underlying problems for those who see class analysis as a tool for understanding power and dehumanization. Of course the "1%"—the top "centile class" in Piketty's schema—came into common usage after Occupy, so it is far from useless as a class concept, capturing something real happening on Wall Street and in the country. But while the idea of the 1% class has already helped fuel a new conversation, "percentile classes" not only "lack a certain poetry" but reflect a problem that Piketty 2 would likely acknowledge: percentile groups do not capture vividly the idea of class as an institutionally rooted group embedded in complex and exploitative relations with other such groups.

That any class identified is "arbitrary" raises the question of whether it actually exists in any sense but a statistical abstraction. Piketty 1 recognizes this, saying that any class he does name—such as the lower class, which he defines as the bottom 50 percent with virtually no wealth, or the upper decile, the top 10 percent that controls most of the wealth—is "quite obviously arbitrary and open to challenge. I introduce these terms," says Piketty, "purely for illustrative purposes, to pin down my ideas, but in fact they play virtually no role in the analysis."[4]

The most serious concern here is whether any new conversation stimulated by Piketty will even discuss class, given the abstract and statistical definition Piketty 1 has given it. It might lead to a new and important conversation about inequality, focusing on the richest Americans and the excesses of their wealth. But this does not lead to describing a class system dehumanizing the mass of workers who have lost control of their work lives and their government. For reasons I examine later, to discuss inequality without discussing class is a major problem. We need to steer the conversation toward a more socially and politically grounded concept of class itself.

That leads to a closely related second problem, the fact that Piketty 1's idea of class, as noted earlier, does not suggest a group with a real social existence or history. Yes, each centile or decile actually represents a group in the population perched somewhere on the income or wealth hierarchy. But a meaningful class is flesh and blood: one with a history, one that has been born or worked in particular institutions such as the factory or office, one that shares certain experiences and consciousness because they occupy a privileged or dispossessed home in the real world.

Whatever one's view of Karl Marx's analysis of classes, virtually everybody could recognize the social reality of the classes he named. Bosses and workers. Owners of capital and those who have nothing but their labor to offer. The capitalists and workers play crucial, visible roles in society and are locked into complex, conflictual relationships with each other that play out in workplaces and communities every day. It is much more difficult to say that about the 14 percent class, the 44 percent class, or the 79 percent class, which are all statistically real but do not necessarily share social roles, institutional positions, and identities. They are just percentiles!

While Piketty 2 is not a Marxist, he would likely see some merit in the way that Marx defined classes. Marx showed how classes form as crucial social actors, wrote about the institutions that breed them, and fleshed out the everyday clashes between them. Even if one rejects Marxism, his classes are anything but statistical abstractions. They represent real people who obviously live and work in different worlds. You know if you're a worker or if you are an owner of a large business—and you know the difference.

Piketty 2 seems to realize the importance of going beyond statistical percentiles. He makes wonderful use of novels by Balzac and Austen to flesh out the real-life stories of the nineteenth-century European wealthy classes who inherited dynastic fortunes and of the working classes who could not succeed no matter how hard they worked. The literary Piketty 2 helps us see the grounded social classes that Piketty 1's percentile definitions miss.

Marx described the history of classes, as real groups of people with a collective story. The working class emerged with the rise of industrial capitalism, born when peasants were thrown off the land by the eighteenth-century British land enclosures, and had nothing but their labor. Marx tells the true drama of the capitalist and working classes as flesh-and-blood historical actors entangled in endless and complex social struggles.[5]

Marx sees classes as groups in the workplace—or system of production—enmeshed in exploitative and dehumanizing relations; the capitalist can only be capitalist by existing antagonistically and exploitatively toward the worker.[6] This central social relation is absent in Piketty 1's statistical concept. None of Piketty 1's percentile classes are defined by their position in the real world of work or production. This may help to explain why there is so little discussion of workers and poor or unemployed people in the book—or of unions and political movements, such as the New Deal, that spoke for the workers, something one would expect from

Piketty 2.[7] This suggests the need to go beyond both Pikettys in a new class discussion, although such a discussion can draw much from Piketty about the concentration of wealth in the 1%, the dominant percentile class that clearly has theoretical utility, social grounding, and popular resonance in America today.

Percentile classes are substantially "desocialized" in the sense that, by definition, they share no institutional position—instead, mainly similar income or assets. Yet we need to qualify this by recognizing that Piketty 1's classes do represent, if not workplace groupings, household groupings that share similar wealth. This leads Piketty, as the British sociologist Mike Savage has pointed out, to intriguing insights about the top decile or 10 percent class, as well as the deciles just beneath it, members of which tend to own their homes, and can expect to pass on to their children household property wealth equal to the lifetime income of the bottom 50 percent of the population.[8] While this shifts attention away from the workplace and away from class conflict, it does illuminate property and home ownership as a new way of socially grounding class, as well as highlighting the role of inherited wealth in the twenty-first-century class system.

There is another qualification to the idea that Piketty's percentile classes are "desocialized." By focusing on wealth, they help undergird a concept of "caste classes," a concept I explore at some depth in the next few chapters. Because wealth is increasingly inherited, looking at classes in terms of distribution of different forms of wealth may highlight the growing role of caste in class divisions and in capitalist society itself. This is where Piketty's work is most original and provocative, and while he doesn't flesh out the utility of his percentile wealth classes for his discussion of caste, we shall soon see that it adds to his strongest contribution: the rise of caste and caste classes in twenty-first-century capitalism, resurrecting earlier forms of caste classes in nineteenth-century American Gilded Age capitalism.

Because of the problems associated with "percentile classes," many neo-Marxists and other politically engaged critics have harshly critiqued Piketty. Some, such as the Marxist David Harvey, as well as the US progressive Keynesian economist James Galbraith, argue that Piketty has no credible concept of capital, partly because his concept of capital includes wealth not part of the means of production, such as personal cars or jewelry. This does take Piketty away from traditional Marxist ideas of capital, but, again, it has potential usefulness as a way to highlight the rise and role of caste.

The capital of caste groups includes all their wealth—whether in production or not. Any analysis of caste society would want to look at all the possessions of the governing castes or caste classes. It is hardly incidental that the rising merchant classes in early capitalism and captains of industry and high-tech up to today have tried to emulate the nobility of earlier aristocratic castes, buying jewelry and artwork as well as building castles and estates replicating those of the nobility. These toys of the capitalist "new money" elites were not factors of production but played an important role in creating the consciousness of who was worthy and constituted part of a superior caste or caste class. We shall return to this theme in later discussions of the role of consumption (see Chapter 11) in patrimonial capitalism, but just note here that the idea of "caste classes" is perhaps the most important contribution of Piketty to ideas about capitalist classes both past and future.

Harvey and Galbraith also critique Piketty's idea of capital because Piketty has no clear way of setting a value on financial assets whose prices may reflect simply a bubble and thus has, in their view, no real way of talking about a capitalist class, its wealth, or a politics of capitalism.[9] The problem in Piketty's definition of capital is not only that it abstracts away from the real-world system of production and thereby makes the "capitalist class" a statistical artifact, but also that it makes it difficult to accurately measure wealth, which will artificially rise during inflationary eras and fall during deflationary ones. How can we know the wealth of any of Piketty's classes, but especially that of the very rich, if his concept of capital reflects vast daily fluctuations of the price of financial assets that have no relation to the stock of physical capital—factories, land, and other factors of production—utilized and valued in the system of production itself?[10]

Focusing on classes based on accumulation rather than workplace divisions, Piketty has unquestionably moved away from a concept of class based on institutional exploitation, something at the heart of Marxist class analysis. Even Keynesian economists, such as Robert Kuttner, who are not Marxists, highlight critically Piketty's neglect of workers and their institutions, such as unions, and of government and its crucial role in worker struggles, as in the New Deal.[11] In other words, most progressives want a concept of class that suggests relations of social control and dehumanization, and they may not find it highlighted in Piketty.

Nonetheless, these critiques, while not lacking merit, can become excessive and disguise the virtues of Piketty's approach. There are theoretical justifications for approaching the concept of class (and of capital) as Piketty does. Regarding, for example, the problem of accurately measuring capital, which is valued on the market and subject to bubbles, the same is true for any concept of capital, whether a factor of production or not. Unless one sticks to an orthodox Marxist labor theory of value, which creates very significant problems of measuring value itself, there is no way of defining capital that doesn't involve problems related to volatility in the market price of all capital assets.

And Marx's concept of class, as with all concepts of classes, has its own problems. For example, Marx's concept of the working class is plagued by problems involving the lack of common consciousness among the many different subgroups of workers, divided by race, gender, and occupation, and the failure of a very large number of workers to see themselves as part of any class at all. Is such a Marxist class—which Marx described as a "class in itself" rather than a "class for itself"—a real social grouping, or just another theoretical construction? And have not Marxists been forced into problematic ideas of "false consciousness" to try to hold together a concept of the working class that does not, at least in the United States, share common views or act with a shared class political agenda? The Marxist working class often attacks its own members—who are members of another biological caste—rather than the class above them, and often seems, as the political writer Thomas Frank shows vividly, to put cultural values of guns, God, and gays above its economic interests. This has led to endless discussions about why US workers appear to act, contrary to Marx, directly against their own class interests, raising questions about the viability of the traditional class concept.[12]

Moreover, Piketty 1—and to some extent Piketty 2—never set out to study class or class warfare, but rather inequality. Piketty acknowledges that his discussions of class are not highly developed and that his statistical aggregates are not intended to provide us with what Marx tried to accomplish: writing the social history and offering a theory of real social groups fighting for justice. Piketty 2 hints at the importance of these issues, and he sometimes fleshes out real class politics in France and Britain, particularly through his dipping into the great nineteenth-century European social novelists.

Moreover, in his discussion of the top centile—the 1% and its various uppermost sections—Piketty 1's class discussion, as noted in Chapter 3, melds with reality and is potentially politically explosive. Occupy protesters saw a 1% acting as a real social class, centered in J. P. Morgan Chase, Bank of America, Goldman Sachs, and other huge Wall Street banks, that organized itself to exploit the 99%. In his analysis of the 1% and of how they accumulate their wealth and power through both super-incomes and inherited wealth, Piketty begins to give scholarly weight to the Occupy political analysis, helping translate statistical abstractions into vivid social reality. In its focus on the 1%, Piketty's book begins to tease out how a percentile class can form as a real social class that accumulates wealth, develops a political agenda, and transforms the entire society. We need to go beyond Piketty 2, though, to truly dissect the 1% and show its structure as a social network advancing a business strategy and serious political agenda that has changed the world. This requires a form of scholarship that political sociologists such as G. William Domhoff, the author of the classic work *Who Rules America,* have already pioneered.[13]

It is noteworthy how much concepts of the 1% and the 99% have taken root in our vocabulary. Admittedly, this is less because of Piketty than Occupy. Nonetheless, the class concepts of the 1% and the 99%—whatever they lack in theoretical sophistication—have already transformed the political conversation. I have seen this in my own courses, where the conversation about the 1% and the 99% immediately lights up the classroom and gets students on the edge of their chairs.

This suggests that Piketty 1's classes, although statistical groupings, are not entirely removed from the social world—and are potentially both conversational game changers and politically powerful. The percentile classes may be statistical abstractions but the 1% and the 99%, at least, are concepts that have the power to capture the imagination of masses of people about how power and inequality operate through a class system. The 1% has brought the idea of class back into everyday conversation, showing that Piketty 1 is speaking a language that can resonate politically.

If you go to the many discussions of French and British literature, you see much more of Piketty 2—and a rich discussion of social classes and the class politics especially of the rich. In his wonderful treatments of novelists such as Honore de Balzac and Jane Austen, Piketty moves from his percentile classes to real social groupings, and his voice becomes that of Piketty 2. Balzac's character Rastignac, an ambitious young man of noble but poor background who is desperate to move upward and live a life of high fortune, learns that no matter how hard he works, he has to marry into inherited great wealth if he wants to realize his dreams. His choice is either to marry a boring heiress and enjoy the aristocratic life or work hard as a lawyer and live a life of middling standing.[14] Jane Austen shows that women not born into wealth have no choice but to marry into landed gentry to live decently—and Piketty's illumination of the unbridgeable gulf between the dynastic aristocracy and those forced to work for a living is even more true of Austen's world than Balzac's, where mobility through work remained possible in parts of the laboring population.[15] Piketty's dive into the literature of Balzac and Austen brilliantly illuminates the aristocratic classes who inherit great wealth, and the working classes (including even working lawyers!) who can never earn enough income to match that dynastic wealth. When Piketty moves into the literary world—a daring adventure for an economist and a reflection of Piketty 2's sensibilities—his book comes to life with the real experiences of real social classes (which are also castes, critical to Piketty's analysis). And even in his nonliterary discussions, such as his extensive discussion of American "super-managers" at the top of Wall Street, his analysis suddenly catches fire. His very tip-top percentile class has the same flesh and blood as Marx's, and reflects Piketty's passion for an economics that is embedded not in mathematical equations but the class struggles of the real world.

The various critiques of Piketty 1 classes all have validity—and show the need to move the post-Piketty conversation beyond Piketty himself. As in much of the book, it is Piketty 1 who has the louder megaphone in discussing classes. But one cannot read his book without hearing also the voice of Piketty 2, entranced by the adventures of Balzac's and Austen's characters and beginning to build an original socially grounded class analysis around them. Moreover, even Piketty 1's approach has caught the attention of an astonishing number of readers and citizens, and we need to revamp our thinking to recognize the power of talking about a few crucial percentile classes: the 1%, the 0.1 percent of the 1%, and the 99%.

Discussion Questions

1. Since the 1% and 99% have a place in the American mind, should we accept Piketty 1's "percentile classes"?
2. How can we move toward Piketty 2's more socially grounded ideas of class in an American conversation?
3. Does the Marxist idea of class have new life in the post-Piketty American conversation?
4. Can we now talk about both class and class warfare and find a large audience in the American public?
5. Is Piketty's concept of class not based on work divisions or on the idea of inherent antagonisms between classes helpful in understanding social differences?
6. How can we know the true wealth of the capitalist class if his concept of capital includes more than the stock of physical capital and involves stocks and bonds that fluctuate every day?
7. Are there old or new American novelists, comparable to Balzac or Austen, who we can read to get insight into the real workings of social class in America?
8. What about Theodore Dreiser in An American Tragedy, one of the most famous American works of literature about a man who lets his fiancée drown because he wants to move up?

5
♦ ♦ ♦

CASTE AND CLASS

What is the relation between caste and class in Piketty's schema? How do race, gender, and inherited privilege figure into our class and capitalist system? Is inherited wealth a form of caste, creating a marriage of caste and class? What are the implications? Will this new thinking change the relation between race, gender, and class movements?

Piketty shows us not just that we need to talk anew about class but that the new class we need to talk about is a recycled version of the old classes of Europe.

This old new class is a "caste class." Piketty is opening a new conversation not only about class but about caste, a concept largely lost in all the commentary on his book, perhaps because he never explicitly uses the term. The idea of caste is historically associated with European feudalism, which envisioned the different castes—the nobility and the serfs—as fundamental different orders of being with distinct essences or bloods. They were assumed to have divinely assigned and genetically and spiritually different human status or essences, with the aristocracy chosen for grace.[1]

Caste today has a slightly different meaning, but it refers to social groups that inherit biological or economic status that cannot be changed over the life course. I define caste as "a status you are born with and will virtually never change."[2] The caste conversation begins to give voice to Piketty 2, because biologically based castes, those based on race and gender, are not abstract wealth percentiles but flesh-and-blood social realities tied in the American mind to real-world struggles. In patrimonial capitalism, economic classes also become castes, based on inherited wealth or poverty, which cannot easily be changed, a theme we develop shortly.

The "caste class" is a major contribution of Piketty's work, because he is changing how we see caste as well as how we need to see class. Americans have been focused on biological and cultural forms of caste, especially race, gender, and sexual orientation. These castes have largely displaced classes in US public discourse and politics. We don't have a strong class conversation in America, but we are mesmerized by the inequalities baked into our skin color, gender, and sexual leaning—and that is what the culture wars and much of our politics are now about.

Castes as we understand them today have given rise to some of the most disruptive and progressive politics of our times, including the civil rights movements, the feminist movement, and the gay movement. While class politics has languished in the United States, caste politics has exploded in what we call "identity politics."[3]

But while such caste or identity politics has been transformative, it has a profound problem: it is largely abstracted from economics and class, and it has largely worked to integrate people into the system rather than overturn it. This has drastically weakened both identity politics and class politics. It reflects the fact that Americans—by essentially abandoning a class conversation—do not see the critical connections between caste and class, between identity movements and class politics. This has created caste movements that have left behind economically disadvantaged women and poor people of color, who are the majorities of their caste. And it has created working-class movements that are split badly by caste, cleaved by color and gender, and thereby drastically weakened and unable to crack the iron hold on economic and political power by the 1% class.[4]

Americans do not see that caste and class have largely melded today, and that the class of the twenty-first century is a "caste class." Caste classes also defined the medieval era (lords vs. serfs) and existed in eighteenth- and nineteenth-century capitalism of the Belle Époque and Gilded Age (lords of industry vs. impoverished workers). This story about Old Europe's "caste classes" occupies much of Piketty's book, reflecting the voices of both Piketty 1 and 2.

Piketty's work shows that classes can also be castes, and that castes have strong class features. In fact, through most of the history of capitalism, classes have been mainly "caste classes." The implications are revolutionary and will be a big part of the new conversation in the twenty-first century.

Start with this basic idea. Castes are groups based on inheritance of any form of social difference that remains relatively permanent or lifelong, whether skin color, gender, or economic privilege.[5] As soon as you add in economic privilege, you realize that caste is not just about biology. Or culture. Caste can also be about economics, and almost always has been, at least by Piketty's account of capitalism.

Piketty's work shows that today, as in nineteenth-century Belle Époque or Gilded Age capitalism, US ruling elites and the working population increasingly fit the definition of castes as well as classes. People inherit not only permanent skin color and gender but, more and more, a lifelong position in the economy. The children of today's 1% "caste class" of top corporate executives will enjoy multimillion-dollar inheritances keeping them rich for life.

American children born into the bottom 50 percent are also becoming a caste class—the majority being female and people of color but also including millions of white males—who earn stagnant, low wages or go jobless. Only about 15 percent get a college degree, the same as their parents, and without this ticket to mobility they also will inherit a relatively permanent dispossessed economic station. The huge lower classes, like the tiny tip-top one, are becoming castes as well as classes.[6]

The idea of "caste classes" helps move us beyond the detached mechanics of Piketty 1 toward the flesh-and-blood social realities of Piketty 2. The caste feature of the class helps ground it in social and political reality. Piketty 1's classes come to life in real social experience and political struggle when translated, with the help of Piketty 2, into identity politics and caste classes.

The role of inherited wealth or capital is at the very center of Piketty's analysis. It shows that capitalism has always been misunderstood, especially in America, as a system of high social mobility and blue sky opportunity.[7] The hardest punch thrown by Piketty's work is its debunking of this mobility idea, which is, after all, the idea of the American Dream. If capitalism is made up of caste classes, groups that have largely inherited a lifelong economic position, then all our thoughts about the American Dream—and about capitalism itself—must change, a subtext of Piketty's book strongly reflecting Piketty 2. We are not leaving the world of caste but entering a new one. And this new caste world—which is also a world of fixed or inherited class positions—can be as harsh as the old, in some ways harsher than in the precapitalist Middle Ages, because today's caste world is mythologized by the language of opportunity, mobility, and meritocracy, leading lower caste classes to blame themselves for laziness or being parasitical and "a taker." At least in medieval feudalism, the lower castes were taught that God had assigned them their station and the aristocratic caste had a divine obligation to care for them.[8]

We need a little historical excursion here to see the complexity of caste and caste ideology in capitalism. Capitalism developed out of feudalism when a new class of merchants who were not part of the nobility arose. They provided valuable goods, such as tea and spices, for the aristocracy, who were living a life of leisure on the land. The merchants had to work for their livelihood, and they created the new capitalist ideology of hard work and merit as part of the new order they were bringing. The feudal aristocracy felt that working demeaned their noble blood or "essence." They looked down on these new merchants who had to work; the aristocracy was a caste too good to work. They were born to play and be supported by others less deserving.

Merchants bringing capitalism into the world rejected the idea that inherited blood or essence elevated an elite class above the need to labor. They claimed—as part of their new capitalist system—that they had earned the right to privilege through their productive work. By the eighteenth or nineteenth century, in the European Belle Époque era of Balzac and Austen, the medieval nobility who saw themselves as too good to work had faded and the new class of mercantile capitalists now ruled in the name of exceptional productivity, based on work and merit.

Piketty's great revelation, though, is that new generations of Belle Époque capitalists were moving, generationally, from being a class of "producers" to being a class of "rentiers," living off inherited fortunes. They continued to claim worth based on their exceptional work and productivity, but they—and their children—were living more like the old feudal aristocracy, who inherited their wealth from their parents and grandparents. They were capitalism's "caste classes," forerunners of what Piketty sees as emerging again today in a new form.

This points to a continuing contradiction about caste in capitalism. The early merchants and then the Belle Époque capitalists still envied the status of the "old money" or "blue blood" families, even if they proudly claimed they had worked for their new wealth, which often exceeded the declining wealth of the old nobility. They wanted to feel that they, too, were fundamentally a superior caste, born with a divinely granted essence. The new capitalist classes were proud of their productivity but also aspired to be new lords of the manor, born to the life of gentry. This conflict between old and new wealth exists still today, with capitalists who "make" their new money coming together in "bohemian groves," as political sociologist G. William Domhoff has described, where they re-create a kind of feudal caste life in their country clubs and manors, defining themselves as superior in breeding and social taste to all others.[9]

Piketty does not discuss this, but it is the cultural side of the economic caste realities in capitalism. Capitalism puts forward a public ideology of postfeudal meritocracy, in which one's fate is determined by hard work and merit rather than birth or inheritance. But, in reality, as Piketty dramatically shows, while many capitalist elites work hard, they are also, in most eras, a "rentier" class that inherits its wealth rather than earns it. Moreover, what this historical interlude has just shown is that they have long harbored the image of themselves as "blue bloods," born to a special breed of select people with the right genes and ancestry. Thus while they broadcast in public the capitalist class ideology of hard work and meritocracy, they also sustain in their private worlds a view of themselves as genetically endowed superior or lordly beings, a kind of biological caste that is a cultural corollary of the inherited wealth and rentier class status that Piketty reveals is their actual economic position.

The implications of Piketty's caste rediscovery are potentially revolutionary. Even Marx felt that capitalism eroded caste as a major social category, replacing it with a postfeudal, postcaste class structure in capitalism. Capitalism, Marx thought, would emancipate people from caste oppression while locking them into class divisions. Piketty's work goes beyond Marx in rediscovering the continuing importance of caste over hundreds of centuries. Capitalism not only does not wipe out biological caste differences but also transports caste into the economic system and melds caste and class. This is perhaps the most intriguing of Piketty's discoveries.

The political implication is profound. Piketty's work has the potential to ignite a new political conversation on the intertwining of caste and class. This could dramatically change our politics, creating new kinds of movements against today's inheritance-based Gilded Age system.

Piketty's analysis hints that "caste class" movements might emerge to challenge a system of inherited privilege. Cultural castes, such as women and African Americans or Hispanics, may increasingly redefine their agenda in terms of the right to economic class gains as well as caste liberation. Already asserting rights to equality based on gender and race, they could ignite a new passion into the struggle for economic rights against inherited lifelong privilege.

If Piketty's predictions about rising inequality and declining mobility prove true, white male workers may see common cause with these fellow caste class members, and increasingly view fair wages, mobility, and economic security as basic rights to protect them against inherited, lifelong economic dispossession. Caste classes could reframe labor struggles as civil rights movements traditionally associated with caste struggles. These themes are not highly developed, because Piketty 1 continues to dominate the volume and Piketty 2 does not flesh out the implications of his analysis for major gender and race caste groups.

Piketty sets the table for a critical examination of the relation of biological caste and a new economic caste system totally intertwined with the class system, but then fails to follow through the implications for the economic position and politics of women, people of color, and gays. I have already argued that the discovery of caste in capitalist economies—and of caste classes—is perhaps Piketty's most important contribution. Yet, commentators have largely ignored the larger implications for gender and race caste groups, and for the politics of caste, perhaps because Piketty himself fails to make the connection.

Let us be clear. Without ever using the term, caste is the most important new concept in Piketty's book. He has shown that capitalism is destined in the current century to be organized around the inherited wealth of the 1% and the lifelong poverty of the disinherited majority, excluded from wealth and power. He has properly put caste back into the heart of the analysis of capitalism, demonstrating that capitalist classes almost always have had strong caste features and seem destined to be a dominating force in the twenty-first century, without major political intervention to change it.

But Piketty then fails to make the connection between the rise of the inheritance principle—and caste—at the center of the economy and its relation to the implications for the biological caste groups of gender and race that Americans have traditionally understood caste to be about. A glance at Piketty's index speaks volumes. There is no reference at all to the word *race* and no mention either of the word *gender*.

What is going on here? Piketty 1, the economist who has brilliantly offered the anatomy of patrimonial capitalism and its organization around the principle of inheritance and inherited wealth, is disassociating from Piketty 2, the sociologist and political scientist, who would instinctively see the potentially explosive relation with biological caste, the other central social system of inheritance. Analytically, even Piketty 1 might have made the association between economic inheritance as the basis of both economic caste and class and the inheritance that defines biological caste. But neither Piketty 1 or 2 makes the connection.

There are at least three problems here. One is that Piketty's analysis of inequality, the heart of his book, fails to flesh out the importance of race and gender in shaping patterns of inequality. The concentration of people of color, and single women especially, in the lower half of the inequality and wealth hierarchies gets almost no attention. We are creating a disinherited majority disproportionately full of people of color and women, even though it also includes white male workers, a potentially crucially important tie between biological and economic castes that have been cultural antagonists. Likewise, the fact that the 1% is overwhelmingly peopled by white men, although it includes of course their wives and daughters, is not highlighted at all. So Piketty has himself excluded biological caste from his analysis of economic caste and class, a major oversight with significant political implications.

Feminists are beginning to recognize this major flaw. Kathleen Geier, in reviewing Piketty's work in the *Nation,* observes that "though *Capital* has many virtues, attention to gender, alas, is not one of them. Like most mainstream economists, Piketty does not deploy gender as a category of analysis, nor does he engage with the work of feminist economists. Nevertheless, he offers insights about the nature of economic inequality that feminists can build on to advance both gender and economic justice."[10] The same precise critique can and must be made about Piketty's failure to use race as an important "category of analysis."

This has led, second, to a relative absence of commentary about Piketty's work by women and people of color. The hundreds of reviews, blogs, and discussions about *Capital in the Twenty-First Century,* at least in the first six months after its publication, almost exclusively involved white males, although as time moves on, more women and people of color are engaging with Piketty's work. The largely white male commentary, though, reinforces the failure to make the connections between biological and economic caste, and help explains the lack of discussion of the political implications of a "caste class" system that brings together, at the bottom, people of color with disadvantaged women and struggling white male workers.

Third, the failure to engage with people of color and women has major political implications. True, Piketty's analysis of the working class as an economic caste, even without reference to gender and race, could mobilize new political movements, if the labor movement, and nonunionized workers more broadly, were to realize the implications of Piketty's analysis. Struggling white male workers buy into the economic system because they continue to believe that hard work and merit offers them a way up the ladder, sustaining faith in the American Dream. If they were to realize that they are now a permanently disinherited class, a lower caste, that would threaten everything about their belief system in the American economic order. So the analysis of inheritance and caste has great significance, even when not tied by white workers to the caste situation of people of color or women.

Nonetheless, even bigger political implications of Piketty's work would come if white workers were to recognize, in their own caste situation, a new recognition of what they share with the biological castes of women and people of color. Both are members of the same "caste class" and now share similar interests in confronting the wealth monopoly and power of the 1%. White male workers may still have biological caste privilege, particularly relating to race, but this may do them little economic good if they are condemned to a low economic position for life. Consciousness of themselves as an economic caste would be a game changer. If white workers saw caste when they looked in the mirror, men with no future, it's possible that they would have a different appreciation of the problems of women and people of color.

Let me note right away, though, that I am not suggesting with any great confidence that white male workers—whatever their awareness of their economic caste position—will act in political solidarity with other members of their "caste class" who are people of color or women. We have too much evidence of failure of the US working class to act in solidarity with others sharing similar economic interests. Piketty's analysis shows that white workers have long shared elements of economic caste with workers of another gender and skin color, without feeling solidarity or acting together on shared interests. In fact, often, quite the contrary is true. The melding of class and class politics is thus simply an intriguing possibility, one important enough to return to in our final chapter, and hopefully will become an important part of the conversation that Piketty's book will spur.

Discussion Questions

1. Will Piketty's book change our idea of caste as a biological rather than economic phenomenon?
2. Will the idea of a "caste class" be understandable and resonate in America?
3. Can we expect a more class-conscious identity politics in America after Piketty?
4. Will women and people of color embrace the idea that they are part of a "caste class" and expand their rights movements to include economic class issues?
5. Will identity politics begin to meld with class politics in America?

THE WORTHY AND UNWORTHY RICH

CLASS AND CASTE IN CAPITALISM

YALE MAGRASS

Piketty points out that capitalism promises equality but fails to deliver. The equality that capitalism allegedly promised was one of opportunity, not of outcome. It may have eliminated caste barriers but class differences would remain. Depending upon your ambition and ability, you can rise or fall from poor to rich. Although Piketty does not use the word *caste*, he suggests the gap between the rich and everyone else is so wide and the possibility of intergenerational mobility so low that capitalism has become essentially a caste society.

Capitalism emerged from feudalism, an explicitly caste society, ruled by the aristocracy, who saw themselves as endowed with a superior essence that biologically separated them from the common lot. In medieval and early modern Catholic theology, they had a grace given to them by God. They were guardians within a "great chain of being," grounded in tradition, in which everyone was interconnected but had an assigned place. The goal was to maintain harmony, order, and stability. As such, progress, trying to uplift oneself, or seeking a profit was shunned. Land had an almost magical quality; so living off of trade or industry was a sign of inferiority. The truly worthy glowed in their essence and their inherited status and need not work.

Capitalists see their workers as "employees," things to use for profit and discard when no long needed. Everyone has their chance. If you fail, you're on your own. On the other hand, aristocrats, as guardians within the great chain of being, were assigned responsibility for those below them. Ironically, aristocratic residues may partly explain why there is greater tolerance for state-supported social services in Europe than America.

The ancestors of the modern capitalist class, also called the bourgeoisie, were medieval wandering merchants who, lacking ties to the land and dependent upon trade, were outside the caste system—outcastes. They were often people with no place within a Christian hierarchy—Jews and Gypsies. However, the Crusades brought aristocrats to crave goods from the East that wandering merchants could bring them and the plagues created labor shortages, which produced a need for more efficient agriculture and calculations for profit. Accordingly, these low lives were now welcome in the courts of the aristocrats. This was the beginning of the transition to capitalism. A class system was emerging parallel to the caste system. Although Piketty does not say this, we can infer from him that caste and class can coexist, but in tension. There can be two simultaneous hierarchies, and you can be on the top of one and at the bottom of the other. In the class system, the low-caste bourgeoisie were now a "middle class," just below the aristocracy. Anxious and insecure about their own status, the rising bourgeoisie had a conflicting attitude toward the aristocracy. They simultaneously saw aristocrats as lazy, parasitical, and incompetent but admired their aura and self-confidence and yearned for their luxurious lifestyle. In prerevolutionary France, some wealthy bourgeoisie bought aristocratic titles. This, of course, raises the question: Were titles really something you had to be born into?

As the bourgeoisie grew in wealth and power, they developed contempt for the aristocracy, came to believe they could rule on their own, and rose up and overthrew the aristocracy though revolutions in England, the United States, and France. To galvanize support, with perhaps some self-deception, they presented the revolutions not as the creation of a new ruling class but of power and freedom for everyone: democracy. They spoke of equality, by which, again, they meant eliminating caste distinctions, not class differences. Using Piketty, we can question if caste was ever overcome, but there were changes. The new democracy would give capitalists the freedom to pursue profit without the restraints of the feudal laws, obligations, and customs. Under feudalism, there were two distinct law codes, courts, and sets of punishments—one for aristocrats and one for commoners. Commoners were legally not allowed to wear certain clothes or colors. Capitalist democracy claims there is one code of justice, which applies to everyone. Now, if you are rich enough, you can do whatever you want. We see the implications of this today in the capitalist interpretation of civil rights. Black millionaires can now buy mansions in formerly all-white gated communities, an ability still unavailable to the vast poor black majority. In precapitalism, castes faced separate means of execution. Aristocrats were beheaded, but commoners were hanged. The French Revolution brought the guillotine, which gave commoners the equal privilege of being beheaded.

The revolutions did not mean the aristocracy would simply vanish. Monarchies would be restored—temporarily in France, and permanently, but without power, in Britain. The two ruling classes, the aristocracy and the bourgeoisie, would simultaneously resist each other, imitate each other, and uncomfortably merge with each other. The surviving aristocrats wanted the capitalists' new wealth and power. At least unconsciously absorbing an inferiority complex from feudalism, many within the bourgeoisie were not completely confident they were worthy of their new dominant position and felt the need to prove they were a select breed, with a superior biological essence and the dignity, manners, airs, and aura of the aristocracy. Sociologist Max Weber suggested that early capitalists, especially before the revolutions, were influenced by a version of Protestantism in which God selects a few and calls them. You had to show you were called, and wealth was a sign of calling. Although capitalists may have been attracted to Protestantism as part of a rejection of the Catholicism of the aristocracy, the idea of calling is very similar to the medieval Catholic concept of grace.

To analyze the culture of early capitalism, Piketty turns to novels by Jane Austen and Honore de Balzac. I am more familiar with Austen. Her novels are mostly about uneasy interactions and romances between capitalists and aristocrats. The aristocrats wanted the capitalists' money, and the capitalists wanted the aristocrats' status. Fiction is a useful tool for understanding cultural values, and Piketty could have considered other authors. Novelist and self-proclaimed philosopher of capitalism Ayn Rand divided the world into two distinct caste classes: creatives and moochers. The creatives are destined to rule and are chosen by some higher, perhaps biological, force (Rand was an atheist who saw religion as a tool of the moochers) but are often held back by the moochers, who can control the state, with disastrous results, allowing the unfit to stand in the way of progress and prosperity. Unions among the creatives would normally breed the most fit children, but sometimes the stork loses his compass and a creative can be born lower on the hierarchy and a moocher can be left on the doorstep of creative parents.

The metaphor of the stork losing his compass is embedded in capitalist ideology. It does not really eliminate the idea of castes with fixed, naturally determined essences. In modern parlance, it can be revealed in DNA. Generally, the children of parents with the stuff necessary to run the corporations and the state will inherit their parents' talent, but the stork does make mistakes. Even some feudal fairy tales are sagas of lost princes and princesses, raised by peasants, goblins, or fairies, who must discover the destiny they were born to and struggle to find their rightful place. Capitalism is an improvement over feudalism because you need equality of opportunity to allow talented children, left on the wrong doorstep, to compete with the children of privilege, prove they have the stuff, rise to their natural station, and achieve their deserved wealth, status, and power. The same competitive process will eliminate rich privileged losers who do not share their parents' gifts and drive.

The fuzzy line between class and caste is apparent in other novelists of early capitalism, upon whom Piketty could have drawn, such as Charles Dickens. *Oliver Twist* is the story of an orphan, abandoned in a workhouse, essentially a slave labor camp where destitute children produce for the wealthy. The inmates must learn their place, not strive to defy nature and rise above it. The director of the workhouse, Mr. Bumble, warns a cook: "Meat, ma'am, Meat. . . . You overfed ma'am. You raised an artificial soul and spirit in him, ma'am, unbecoming to a person of his condition." Oliver Twist does advance but not because of any personal achievement. It turns out he literally was left on the wrong doorstep and was the great-nephew of wealthy Mr. Brownlow, whose pregnant niece, having shamed the expectations of her "class caste," ran to a workhouse where she gave birth and died. Oliver's status is restored when he is readmitted to his great-uncle's family.

Horatio Alger is considered the Gilded Age author of the American Dream, whose worthy, ambitious characters rise from "rags to riches." However, even in his novels, his characters do not necessarily rise because they work or achieve on their own, but sometimes because of in-born family worth. Like Oliver Twist, Mark the Match Boy is another orphan left on the wrong doorstep. He also joins the upper-caste class when he is discovered by his rich uncle. One lesson you can glean from these novels is that capitalist ideology does not really abandon the idea of innate essences but retains it, although in a somewhat more subtle, convoluted form than in feudalism.

Merely having money is not enough to prove you are among the select. The bourgeoisie felt a need to show they were at least as deserving as the aristocracy, whom at one level they denounced, but on another level, they envied. Capitalists had to prove they were worthy, and the aristocracy still provided the standard to which they appealed. Even today, Americans are obsessed with the British royal family. For centuries, a distinction has been made between the worthy poor, who try to work and are victims of circumstances beyond their control, and the unworthy poor, who are lazy parasites. There is also a distinction between the worthy and unworthy rich, but it has almost opposite criteria to those applied to the poor. The worthy rich come from good OLD families, have grace and manners, dress properly, show good taste, and appreciate fineries like vintage wines. They may display precious jewelry, whose primary use is to be able to say, "I am rich enough to spend money on something useless." Once established, they are beyond pecuniary pursuits and can spend their time in elegant leisure. Some among the worthy rich work, but they do so voluntarily, not because they need the money but because as the chosen, they are guardians of society, doing their duty. The unworthy rich are nouveau riche, impertinent upstarts, just barely earning their fortunes, who have to work to maintain and grow their wealth, lack grounding in society, and are ignorant of the rules of proper etiquette. They are self-made and come from low families. They can be Jews, Italians, Irish, and even blacks or Asians.

Gilded Age political economist Thorstein Veblen proposed a *Theory of the Leisure Class*, who, once establishing themselves, focus on proving their worthiness for the status through leisure, conspicuous consumption, and elegant entertainment. Despite the contempt the European or American bourgeoisie may have expressed for the aristocracy, the aristocracy remained the bourgeoisie's model as the capitalists tried to emulate the lords and dukes. There was no such contempt among antebellum Southern slave owners who ran their plantations to openly replicate European feudal manors. In the post–Civil War Gilded Age, Northern industrialists and financiers, having defeated the South, now tried to prove their worth did not come from mere money, but that they, too, had grace and elegance and were a true aristocracy.

In a generation, there could be a shift from new to old money. Cornelius Vanderbilt, the Commodore, who built the New York Central Railroad, was a crude, vulgar, uneducated sea captain, who made blunt remarks like, "What I care about the law? Hain't I got the power." His children and their descendants became the epitome of "high society." Amy Vanderbilt wrote one of the definitive guidebooks on etiquette. Even if the Commodore's son, William, ran the railroad from his office in Grand Central Station, his family entertained the worthy rich with lavish elegant parties in the "cottages" of Newport, Rhode Island, which were deliberately built to imitate European aristocratic palaces like Versailles.

To be among the worthy rich, you had to have not only material capital but also what French sociologist Pierre Bourdieu, whom Piketty admires, called *cultural capital,* manners and refinement indicative of membership within a select caste. You have to know the proper order of knifes, forks, and spoons and know which knife is for meat and which is for fish. Even European aristocrats who lost their material capital retained their cultural capital. Indeed, their cultural capital came from the mere fact that they were from an old aristocratic family, no matter what they themselves did or how they behaved. Gilded Age rich American families often would send their children to study and live in Europe and acquire the veneer of the aristocracy. Sometimes, the sons of American capitalists would marry the daughters of poorer European aristocrats and acquire their wives' title and status. The daughters of rich Americans would attend "finishing schools" to learn the manners needed to "come out" as debutantes in high society.

The codes of dress, style, and behavior among the worthy rich are deliberately so subtle that when they are followed, they may not be recognized by outsiders. They are signals to the fellow worthy rich that "I am one of you." If you cannot realize when the code is being followed, that is proof that you do not have the right stuff. New Money people, who do not fully understand the code, can be too conspicuous in trying to imitate Old Money people. If you can be detected, that is indication that you are among the unworthy rich. The worthy rich travel in an exclusive circle for which mere money does not qualify its members. There are clubs, resorts, and communities for which your whole background must be examined before you can be admitted. Outsiders may not even know they exist. Ivy League universities have secret societies. The fact that I know about them makes me wonder how secret they are. At Yale, there is Skull and Crossbones, to which both President Bushes and John Kerry belonged. Being academically selected to attend Yale does not qualify you for "Skull and Cross." You have to be from the right family, with the right background, the right kind of money, and the right airs and manners.

The aristocracy are aware that they are the embodiment of high society; as they sing in the musical My Fair Lady:

> Every duke and earl and peer is here.
> Everyone who should be here is here.

Piketty uses novels to illustrate his point, but movies can also work, especially movies that fictionalize real events. The conflict between the worthy and unworthy rich permeates the 1997 film Titanic—a great metaphor. The Titanic sank at the end of the Gilded Age. One passenger is Molly Brown, a real historical person, who is the vulgar wife of a low-born but very rich miner from Denver. In another movie about her, The Unsinkable Molly Brown, she goes to Europe without her husband specifically to learn aristocratic manners, but she decides she does not belong and sails home on the Titanic. Molly Brown lacks proper airs and has not learned how to be pretentious. In the film Titanic, she sits in the first-class dining room at a table full of worthy rich, who shun and mock her. As a reward for having rescued Rose DeWitt Bukater, a fictional first-class passenger, working-class Jack Dawson (also fictional) is invited to sit at the table of worthy rich. Molly lends Jack her son's tuxedo and warns him that he's going into the "snake pit." Jack is actually a talented artist who, despite his poverty, was able to study in Paris. Rose is a rich girl whose family lost their money but still has social status. Her mother is pressuring her to marry rich, pompous Cal Hockey (fictional), who has both wealth and status. Cal may be bourgeois but he identifies with the aristocracy. He proclaims, "We are royalty, Rose," members of a superior lot who have a special, essentially biological, stuff that separates them from riff-raff like Jack Dawson, no matter how much artistic talent Dawson may have. Transcending her caste-class background and disgusted with the likes of Cal and her mother, Rose falls in love with

Jack. Rose survives the sinking of the ship; Jack does not. Had he lived, he might have succeeded and become a distinguished artist, not because of his talents, genuine as they might have been, but because of Rose's far more important connections.

Piketty suggests that in the Gilded Age (called the Belle Époch in Europe), the gap between the rich and everyone else was so profound that elite was as much a caste as a class. He proposes that inequality somewhat diminished from 1920 to 1980, but it has grown so much since then that we have entered a new Gilded Age. The evidence he presents is convincing, and it appears he is right. Piketty writes that one difference between today's elite and that of the Gilded Age is that today's upper caste class work, but William Vanderbilt, Andrew Carnegie, and John D. Rockefeller certainly worked, and today, there are people like Paris Hilton. She parties. She is a celebrity because of her looks and her name, but she probably has never sat behind a desk or managed a hotel. People who collect stock dividends and know nothing about the corporations they effectively own are likely to become even more common in the next generation and may become as prevalent as they were during the Gilded Age. Increasingly, they live in armed gated communities and are becoming more isolated from ordinary people than the French nobility who were sheltered in Versailles. The prognosis seems to be one predicted by Veblen and one with which Piketty will likely agree. Capitalism will mutate into a new feudalism, and caste barriers will grow more profound. Unlike the old aristocracy, the new one has adopted capitalist ideology, which exempts them from the responsibility of taking care of the rest of society. Resources will be destroyed and lives ruined to provide luxuries for the chosen few. As Piketty says, all is contingent. There is no way of knowing how long such a state can be sustained. Maybe there will be new dark ages or maybe social movements can force a transformation. I will not claim any predictive power.

6

♦ ♦ ♦

THE PROBLEM WITH MARKETS

Has Piketty opened up a new conversation on American capitalism, and is it different from what the economics profession has taught? Is he offering us a new vision of how our market system actually works? Do markets—and what are markets, anyway?—actually play the central role that economists define in capitalism? How much does the "free market" shape the economy, and does it really exist? Does the market actually determine prices and wages, or is it social norms and political power that makes these crucial determinations? Does the new post-Piketty conversation change our basic view of capitalism?

Piketty almost certainly meant his book to spark a new conversation about capitalism. He chose a title designed to evoke Karl Marx, whose most famous work is entitled *Das Kapital*.[1] This has given right-wing critics red meat to dismiss Piketty as a Marxist dressed up in new clothes, a man seeking to demonize capitalism and transform our benign views of how it worked. But the truth is quite different, although the right-wingers are not entirely wrong.

Piketty is explicit that he is not a Marxist; in fact, he claims not to have read much of Marx's work. His rejection of Marxism does not mean, of course, that he has no interest in creating a new conversation about capitalism. Piketty showers the reader with profoundly interesting and original insights about how our capitalist system operates. But before getting to that, let us be emphatically clear that Piketty himself, and especially Piketty 1, does not view capitalism as his central concern. He has written a book about inequality. That is quite different than writing a book about capitalism.

Marx himself saw gaps in wages as something of a distraction. Marx sometimes supported workers organizing for higher wages or other benefits, but reducing the gap was far from his major concern.[2] Higher wages might even gild the capitalist lily, obscuring the deeper problems with capitalism itself. These had less to do with income inequality gaps than with the alienating system of work and production, which stripped workers of their autonomy and dispossessed them of power and dignity by putting the entire economy in private hands. Ultimately, capitalism threatened their jobs, with no survival recourse since they did not own the means of production. Reducing income or even wealth inequality gaps would have only a modest impact on these structural injustices of capitalism and thus received relatively little of Marx's attention. To be clear: reducing inequality does not imply any major structural change in capitalism. It keeps capitalism intact, but simply redistributes its fruits, a point that the historian Russell Jacoby has made insightfully in his commentary on Piketty.[3]

Jacoby's comments are memorable:

> Equality figures little in the works of Marx. He never thought that the wages of the workers could get very high, but even if they did reach a modest height, that was not the point. The deadening work remained, no matter the wages. Capital dictated the parameters, rhythms and definition of work, what is profitable and what is not. Even under "easy and liberal" capitalism, where the worker gets better wages and can enlarge his enjoyments and consumption, his situation does not fundamentally change. Better pay no more alters his dependence "than do better clothing, food and treatment, and a larger *peculium* [savings] in the case of a slave." At best, higher wages mean that "the length and weight of the golden chain the wage-laborer has already forged for himself allow it to be loosened somewhat."[4]

While Jacoby's comments are dead on, Piketty's focus on inequality, nonetheless, leads him to basic new insights about capitalism. If Piketty had little to say new about capitalism, the "Piketty phenomenon" probably would not have occurred. Plenty of other excellent volumes on inequality—by other brilliant Keynesian economists, such as Joseph Stiglitz and Robert Reich—had already been written, creating wide readership and important public discussion but nothing like the Piketty phenomenon.[5]

Piketty sheds light on inequality by telling us original things about how capitalism operates as a system, while also offering surprising and provocative new insights into how markets work. And he points toward a rather different view of capitalism than most Americans—and most American economists—have seen. He tells us that capitalism is as much a social and political system as an economic one, and that markets will act differently in different societies because of varying social values and norms. Just as important, the outcomes of capitalist systems are determined as much by social and political power as by efficient or "free" markets. Moreover, with the help of his far-reaching historical data, he offers new and disturbing evidence about the relation between capitalism and inequality in the long term. Perhaps most explosive, he shows that capitalism over many centuries is as much about inherited wealth as it is about equal opportunity and hard work. This is true of both Pikettys, but if we were to follow Piketty 2 to the edge of his thinking and beyond, we would find not just a new vision of capitalism but a critique that has certain strong similarities with Marx. That is the sense in which his right-wing critics are not entirely wrong.

What, then, are the new questions and conversation about capitalism that bubble up from Piketty's work? The broadest is the question about whether capitalism is a fair system, offering opportunity and prosperity to all. Is it a system prone to distribute its fruits widely and to lift the standard of living of the great majority of the population over the long term, or does it unfairly restrict the creation of wealth to a tiny minority?

Piketty rejects here both the neoclassical sunny view of Adam Smith and Milton Friedman and the apocalyptic view developed by Marx.[6] Neoclassical economics—which dominates the American economics profession—sees Smith's "invisible hand" of the market as tending to ensure that capitalism promotes the general welfare in the long run.[7] By encouraging all to pursue their own self-interest, the markets will benefit the most talented and hardest working, whose creativity and entrepreneurial wealth will trickle down to help most of the rest of the population. The result will not be an equal society, but a just and generous one ensuring that the most worthy and deserving succeed and that most others will prosper. Capitalist prosperity will trickle down and benefit the vast majority.[8]

Piketty's historical data directly challenge this optimistic assumption. Over the past two centuries, in many developed European countries and in the United States, the invisible hand turns out to be not only invisible but absent. While a few do get very rich, it is questionable whether it is because of their talents or because they were born "on third base," into wealthy families (just enough of those born low move up to make the mobility myth still seem real to many workers). Moreover, the great majority of the workers have not typically seen a significant trickle-down effect, with the gap between the rich and everyone else large and now growing. The well-being of the society at large is threatened, not only by chronic inequality but by the wastefulness of the wealth produced and the vital public goods that are squandered or never created, an idea not highly developed in the book but clearly evident in Piketty 2.

Beyond the question of the justice and prosperity that capitalism breeds, Piketty raises other disquieting questions about how capitalism and markets actually operate. The conventional neoclassical economics view is that markets allocate resources efficiently because of competition and the adjustment of supply to demand. In contrast to government-run economies, in which the state allocates resources and determines prices and wages, capitalism is a free system in which markets makes these decisions impersonally and impartially. Nobody is coerced and there is no central power—whether in the state or the market itself—controlling the economy. The magic of the market is that it operates rationally, not through the decisions of a few people with power but rather in response to the voluntary decisions made by millions of producers, workers, and consumers.[9]

Piketty raises serious challenges to this reigning theory of capitalist markets, although he does not entertain the core Marxist argument that the market is created by and for powerful elites at the expense of everyone else. But Piketty does raise the extremely important question of power: the idea of mainstream economics that nobody is in charge of capitalist markets. This challenge to conventional economic wisdom is voiced most strongly by Piketty 2 but also argued in more limited contexts by Piketty 1. Because the point is made most clearly in Piketty's discussion of the labor market—and how wages are determined among the highest-paid employees—I will use it as the primary example.[10]

Conventional economics uses the theory of marginal productivity to explain capitalist labor markets and wages. The idea is that the wage or income of each worker or employee will be determined by the contribution of that worker to the added value of the firm in a particular year. Essentially, the market matches the marginal productivity of the worker to his or her compensation, thus offering a "scientific" basis for the idea that differences or inequalities in wages are justified because they reflect differences in worker productivity.[11]

Piketty offers a devastating critique of this perspective, arguing that, at least when it comes to the pay of people at the very top, the theory of marginal productivity is sheer "ideology" rather than science. Estimating the productivity of top executives, Piketty argues, is "impossible."[12] Senior managers in large firms are carrying out unique tasks that are political as well as economic—and whose contribution to the firm can never be scientifically assessed or measured. Sorting out the added value they create—which is inextricably related to value created by hundreds or thousands of workers below them—is a fool's errand. Nonetheless, by claiming that managerial pay reflects productivity, the firm and top employees not only justify their own extravagant compensation but legitimate the entire labor market and capitalism itself.[13]

Here, Piketty begins to challenge, if not entirely unravel, the entire economic and moral foundation of the economists' market theory—and of their embrace of capitalism. If productivity does not and cannot determine the pay of senior managers, what does? Well, not surprisingly, the decisions about their worth are made by the corporate top managers themselves. Their salaries, says Piketty, "are set by the executives themselves. . . . It may be excessive to accuse senior executives of having their hands 'in the till,' but the metaphor is probably more apt than Adam Smith's metaphor of the market's 'invisible hand.'"[14]

Piketty does not entirely dismiss the economists' productivity argument. For routine or relatively unskilled work, he writes (and this is the voice especially of Piketty 1), "As in the case of an assembly-line worker or fast-food server, we can give an approximate estimate of the 'marginal product' that would be realized by adding one additional worker or waiter (albeit with a considerable margin of error in our estimate)."[15] Piketty 1 goes on to say that the theory of marginal productivity "offers a plausible explanation of the long-run evolution of the wage distribution, at least up to a certain level of pay and within a certain degree of precision."[16] Here, Piketty 1 accepts the idea that the labor market sets wages in relative, if imprecise, relation to the productivity of workers at the lower skill levels, and he refuses to throw all of market theory out the window.

But Piketty has opened a Pandora's box for economists in his account of senior managers. For suddenly he has introduced the idea of power—and the view that it is managerial politics more than market forces that dictate important compensation packages in capitalist societies. Deciding wages "is a process [yielding] decisions that are largely arbitrary and dependent on hierarchical relationships and on the relative bargaining power of the individuals involved."[17]

While this may seem almost obvious, it is the beginning of a more expansive discussion that no doubt inspires dread in conventional economists and cracks open the American capitalist consensus. For it is the opening salvo of a larger critique by Piketty 2 of the most basic ideas of economists about the market. Piketty 2 writes that "the labor market is not a mathematical abstraction whose workings are entirely determined by natural and immutable mechanisms and implacable technological forces; it is a social construct based on specific rules and compromises."[18]

Ouch. "A social construct." Piketty 2 is defining the market as a social construction, something that varies from society to society because people write the rules and power dictates outcomes. For an economist, this is something like the pope denying the divinity of Jesus. It takes market economics out of physics—and out of economic science itself—and puts it squarely in history, sociology, and politics. Here, Piketty 2 is approaching heresy about markets—and about capitalism, which is the structure of the larger market system.

To reinforce the point, Piketty 2 brings down the hammer on economists' labor market theory in another way: "Wage hierarchies ... are very difficult to explain solely in terms of the supply of and demand for various skills."[19] In other words, the supply and demand factors that economists enshrine as almost divine forces—outside of human control—are not determining the way the markets operate.

Piketty is suddenly taking seriously his own introductory view that economics is not only not physics but not just economics. When thinking of the capitalist labor market, especially as it operates among managers, power and social norms play an enormous role: "These social norms reflect beliefs about the contributions that different individuals make to the firm's output and to economic growth in general. Since uncertainly about these issues is great, it is hardly surprising that perceptions vary from country to country and period to period and are influenced by each country's specific history."[20] Piketty 2 continues, "The problem is now to explain where these social norms come from and how they evolve, which is obviously a question for sociology, psychology, cultural and political history, and the study of beliefs and perceptions at least as much as for economics per se."[21]

The heresy becomes stark. Piketty 2 writes that "in practice, the invisible hand does not exist, any more than 'pure and perfect' competition does, and the market is always embedded in specific institutions such as corporate hierarchies."[22] In the real world, market equations fade dramatically, and human beings exercising power and social values—which vary enormously from society to society—take over. Of course, conventional economists recognize that in practice the world doesn't perfectly behave according to their theoretical equations. But Piketty is going further, explicitly arguing that the theory itself is fundamentally flawed because it leaves out all the historical, sociological, and political forces that have to be part of any sensible theory of economics. He is also showing that the gap between economic theory and the real world is startlingly large, far larger than most economists would admit. This backs up his personal indictment at the beginning of his book that economists in the United States, while feeling like gods, understand virtually nothing about the real economy, something he also recognized about himself when he practiced the American mathematical economic approach.[23]

What is going on here? Piketty 2 is starting a conversation—that both social scientists and millions of citizens needs to pursue and expand—about market theory as more an "ideology," in his words, than a science. The implication for economics is dire; since he claims that clever economists know "virtually nothing about anything," he is arguing that the discipline must be reinvented. Universities need to be deeply involved because their current intellectual approach and departmental divisions among the social sciences and humanities undermine the understanding of the real social world in the name of detached science.

And Piketty 2 is not shy about making clear that he realizes this is more than an academic debate but an ideological struggle around defining the morality of the market and capitalism. He writes that the entire theory of marginal productivity is an ideological weapon, in the case of the enormous incomes given to top managers, which becomes "a justification for higher status" and justifies astonishingly high income, sometimes in the hundreds of millions of dollars.[24] It is a justification for the existence of the 1% itself.

The conversation we need beyond Piketty involves taking Piketty 2's critique of market theory and seeing how far it applies not just to the legitimation of extravagant 1% salaries but to the entire market system, and to capitalism itself. As we show later, the problem of defining productivity exists across most of the labor force, and the judgment about what kind of skill and contribution made by any worker is always determined by relativistic and somewhat arbitrary social and cultural subjective criteria, often imposed by elites and easily seen as in their interests. One can easily argue that workers who are seen as "low productivity," such as aides in nursing homes, are required to do some of the most complex and demanding physical and emotional work. And those who work behind desks on many corporate suites, as shown in *The Wolf of Wall Street*, are not necessarily spending all their time working inexhaustibly or with impeccable discipline and skill. In other words, we can move beyond even Piketty 2 and reasonably argue that the entire labor market—and all wages—are significantly reflecting cultural biases and power rather than any rational assessment of productivity.

This calls into question the efficiency of the market and the concept of the invisible hand, because the hand of power is operating at every level of the market. If there is no "invisible hand," then the moral foundation of neoclassical market theory—and of capitalism—begins to collapse. This conversation needs to go far beyond where Piketty takes it, to the vast externalities built into all markets, leading to social and environmental costs that the market does not see or correct, and in turn leading to moral and existential catastrophes such as climate change. Piketty's failure to discuss externalities and the broader crises and failures of markets is a significant limitation. His work requires an extended discussion of today's most serious problems of climate change and war. It also requires a careful critique of mainstream economists' failure to distinguish between what is valuable on the market and what is value for society. His failure to follow through on these critiques is a reason that many progressives may unfortunately dismiss his work, despite the key insights it offers.

Of greatest importance, Piketty's analysis does tell us that we cannot and should not assume anything about the moral legitimacy of the market because it is embedded in and operates by the rules dictated by the social, cultural, and political systems of each society. In patrimonial capitalism, the 1% creates and benefits from the markets it helps structure, by virtue of its inherited wealth and power. Whether the market—which is different in different societies—is moral and legitimate, then, is really a question about the legitimacy of the power of elites and the social values of each society. It is a question for sociologists, historians, political analysts, and, most important, ordinary citizens, and one that economists can claim no special authority on. Their "economic science" of capitalism's magical invisible hand proves to be simply a magical illusion, disguising what should be realistically seen by all citizens as a "visible hand" of social classes and power elites. Beyond Piketty is a new conversation about capitalism that becomes essential in the twenty-first century of an ever more globalized and unequal class-based society.

Discussion Questions

1. How has Piketty changed our understanding of markets?
2. Do you agree that the salaries of the 1% are "inside jobs," set by the 1 percenters themselves?
3. If salaries do not reflect the productivity of top managers, do you think that the wages of ordinary workers reflect their productivity? If not, what determines them?
4. Do you understand what Piketty means when he says that markets are "social constructions"—driven by social mores and political power as much as by supply and demand?
5. How does this huge role of social and political factors—and the idea of markets as social constructions—undermine the conventional economic understanding of markets?
6. Has Piketty changed our understanding of capitalism? What are the implications of his argument that Adam Smith's "invisible hand" is a myth?
7. How do Piketty 1 and Piketty 2 disagree about the way markets operate—and what do they agree on? How would Karl Marx respond to Piketty 1 and Piketty 2?

7

♦ ♦ ♦

EXTREME INEQUALITY AND
THE EINSTEIN FORMULA

*How much inequality exists in America, and how does it compare historically
and today with other developed capitalist societies? How can we explain rising
and very high inequality in most capitalist countries through most of history? Is
extreme inequality inherent in the capitalist system? Does it change our conception
of what capitalism is all about? Does it suggest that Marx may have been more
right than most Americans have thought?*

In one of my classes on political economy, I start with an exercise. I
line up five students near the front of the class, each standing next to
each other and representing 20 percent of the population (a "quintile"). I add a sixth student to the line, representing the top 1%! I then
ask them to take steps forward or backward reflecting the change in the
average real household income of their quintile over the past twenty-five
years. They move a step backward for each 10 percent decline (so if their
income has declined 30 percent they take three steps backward, take
no steps if their income has not changed, and move a step forward for
each 10 percent increase; if their quintile average income has increased
40 percent they take four steps forward). What happens? The lowest or
poorest quintile steps back about a step; the second-lowest and middle
both barely move forward, about half a step, the second-highest quintile
moves almost four steps forward, and the richest 20 percent about seven
steps forward. But what really gets the students' attention is the top 1%,

who moves forward about eleven steps—and sometimes I add the top .01 percent, who moves so many steps forward that this student has to leave the room and go to the next building on campus.[1]

This exercise draws a vivid picture of inequality in America. It sticks in the mind—and students who graduate often tell me they remember it more than anything else in the class. What does this picture tell them, I ask. Put simply: the poor get poorer and the rich get much, much, much richer. The majority stagnate. In more detail: they say that the poor get poorer and the second-poorest group and the middle go nowhere (this means that 60 percent of the population, while working longer and more jobs over the past quarter century, are seeing essentially no growth in their income). The top quintile is pulling away, but it is the top 1% (and its top 1 percent) that is visual dynamite. The very rich are getting so much richer than everyone else that the exercise gets them to move up out of the room entirely. They are on a different planet.

Piketty's book is about inequality, and it provides the solid data behind what students describe as a shockingly depressing picture. After the exercise, they joke they need Prozac. Because of the overwhelming data Piketty has collected, and the way he organizes the data, he has forever changed the way Americans and the world will think about inequality. Those who read him will probably all feel they need a strong dose of an antidepressant—except, of course, those born into the 1%.

The data are staggering but are consistent with what we have learned from many other recent studies of inequality—and do not create a revolution in our thinking about the reality of big income and wealth gaps, although the analysis is strikingly original in discussing how such extreme inequality is created, transmitted, and enhanced from generation to generation. More revolutionary is Piketty's analysis of the history of inequality—and its likely future. Extreme inequality, he shows, has characterized most developed capitalist countries over the past two to three centuries, and seems destined to get even more extreme this century. Throughout capitalist history, declining inequality and greater equality occur only in rare periods. This appears to turn our conventional picture of capitalism upside down: Piketty's capitalism is a system of chronic vast inequality, a picture at odds with the consensual economists' view, as noted earlier, that the market economy tends to be a rising tide that lifts all boats. [2]

While we explain this upheaval in the view of capitalism shortly, let us look first simply at the inequality facts. The defining feature of

America today is its extreme inequality of income, and especially income from labor (the income you get from your wages or paycheck). The top 10 percent in America receive about half of all income in the United States and is on track, if current trends continue, to "set a new record around 2030 … about 60 percent of national income while the bottom half would get barely 15 percent."[3]

Income can come from either returns to capital (rent from land, dividend from stocks, etc.) or labor (wages). What is record-breaking about the United States today is the inequality associated with income from labor. Piketty, who is not prone to exaggeration, makes an astonishing assertion: "What primarily characterizes the US at the moment is a record level of inequality of income from labor (probably higher than in any other society at any time in the past, anywhere in the world including societies in which skill disparities were extremely large.)"[4]

Digest these words. *The United States has more inequality of labor income—inequality in the amount of money people make from working—than any society in the history of the planet.*

The reasons seem pretty clear. While most Americans' wages have been stagnant over the past few decades, the pay of executives in big companies has been skyrocketing to a level never seen before. Top executives, or "super-managers," as Piketty calls them, are nailing higher salaries—in the tens of millions of dollars per year—than anyone in history. The United States has virtually invented this new super-paid income class of corporate elites, an innovation that seems, to say the least, morally dubious. Piketty indicates that multimillion-dollar salaries may be more than workers or the general population can handle without revolting, perhaps because they will be left with so little of the national income that they won't be able to fill their own stomachs.

The top 1% currently takes about 20 percent of American national income. This is double, triple, or quadruple the amount that the 1% takes in continental European countries. In Sweden, the top 1% takes about 4 percent rather than 20 percent of the income pie. If this extreme redistribution of pay upward continues in America, according to current trends, "a revolution," writes Piketty, "will likely occur."[5]

He continues, "When it comes to the ownership of capital, such a high degree of concentration is already a source of powerful political tensions."[6] This turns us to the subject of wealth rather than income. Wealth or ownership of capital (such as land, homes, and especially stocks and bonds) is always far more unequal than inequality of income—in every society. While America is historically unique because of its extreme inequality of labor income relative to any other country, even that inequality pales in terms of American wealth inequality.

We've heard the data before, but they never cease to shock. In the United States in 2010–2011, the top 10 percent owned 72 percent of America's wealth. The top 1% owned 35 percent, of which the top 1 percent of the 1%—families of billionaires such as the Waltons, Kochs, Gateses, and Buffets—owned a hugely disproportionate share. And as Piketty indicates, this is self-reported wealth collected by Federal Reserve surveys, which "underestimates the largest fortunes." So the very uppermost reaches of the 1% class—*only a few hundred or thousand families*—who hide their wealth in foreign bank accounts, trusts, and other mysterious "dark money" assets, may actually own something like 30 percent or more of America's wealth. This is far, far more than the entire bottom 50 percent of Americans have, who own only 2 percent of their country's wealth.[7]

Piketty concludes, "For millions of people (the bottom half—160 million people in the US), 'wealth' amounts to little more than a few weeks' wages in a checking account or low-interest savings account, a car, and a few pieces of furniture. The inescapable reality is this: wealth is so concentrated that a large segment of society is virtually unaware of its existence."[8]

Piketty says that if the current inequality trends continue, by 2030 the top 1% will own 50 percent rather than 35 percent of the nation's wealth. Again, he argues that a revolution is likely to happen if this is not reversed.[9]

How does one explain such huge inequality gaps, which Piketty says are likely to accelerate in the twenty-first century? This gets into the truly important issues: What is capitalism really all about? Marx says there are no surprises here: capitalism is a system rigged to funnel money to a tiny super-wealthy capitalist class that will ultimately bring on a revolution against itself organized by desperately impoverished workers. Is Piketty saying the same thing?

Piketty 1 would say no, and Piketty 2 would also lean against making too much of the apparent similarities with Marx, who also—albeit with far more certainty—predicted the possibility of revolution against owners of capital by workers. But even if the analysis is different—and

Marxist and Piketty concepts of capital and class differ in many ways, as already discussed—there are similarities worth highlighting that could make the current century post-Piketty conversation seem something like a seminar led by Marx's ghost.[10]

Let us note first that Piketty says there are only two ways to achieve the extreme inequality we find in a nation like the United States. The first is through a "hyper-patrimonial society" or "society of rentiers" in which, as Piketty explains, "inherited wealth is very important and where the concentration of wealth attains extreme levels."[11] The second way is when extreme unequal societies are organized such that "the peak of the income hierarchy is dominated by very high incomes from labor rather than inherited wealth."[12] Piketty argues that American inequality is more of the second form; in fact, it virtually invented it, through the cleverness and power of its tip-top 1% of "super-managers" or top corporate executives who pay themselves literally a fortune. Yet Piketty acknowledges that the inequality logic of inheritance and super-income payments can exist together in a very unequal society like the United States. "The two types of inequality can coexist: there is no reason why a person can't be both a super-manager and a rentier," and he believes many corporate barons at the upper reaches of the 1% in the United States today are both.[13]

Piketty's arguments about inheritance, so central to his book, in some ways make capitalism—and its extreme inequality—seem even less moral than Marx did. Marx recognized that early capitalists often came from wealthy landed nobility, and that capitalist successes might lead to vast inherited wealth. But inheritance was not the true capitalist path. Capitalists invented, wrangled, or stole their wealth through their own insidious initiatives. It wasn't virtuous, but at least it reflected surviving and thriving on their own (often sociopathic) wits, not those of their parents. To the extent capitalists inherited their wealth, they were following a precapitalist model from the medieval world of feudal aristocracy. Marx saw that world as far more exploitative and oppressive than the world of capitalism.[14]

Piketty's arguments about inequality deriving from super-high incomes are actually more consistent with Marx's views about capitalism. Marx saw the income of capitalists as coming mainly from capital (in the form of interest and profit from their stocks) rather than from their salary packages (although much of their salary comes in stock options and bonuses). Marx did not emphasize the phenomenon of executive managerial salaries. But Piketty's account of how super-managers manipulate their boards to pay them their astronomical compensation is entirely consistent with how Marx saw the operation of capitalism, that is, as a power grab, with the capitalists making and rigging the rules. Piketty's account of the labor market—and markets in general—as social constructions and political muscle are entirely aligned with the Marxist account. The super-managers don't make tens of millions of dollars because of their high productivity but because they have power to set their own compensation. Marx would certainly agree and also view inequality as less the invisible hand and more the "hand in the till."

Piketty's other primary contribution—his historical revelation that capitalism almost always breeds extreme inequality—is central to his book, and it raises other striking comparisons with Marx. Recall that Piketty's core finding is that capitalism over at least the past two to three hundred years—as well as across most developed capitalist countries—gives rise to very high inequality. In his historical approach and his conclusion, Piketty starts a new conversation that converges very closely with Marx. But his reasoning and explanation for perpetual capitalist inequality—to the extent he offers a clear theory—is less similar to Marx and less apocalyptic, but nonetheless more similar than appears on the surface.

Piketty's most widely discussed finding is that capitalist societies are almost all characterized by high inequality in almost all periods. The only big exception in modern times is in the mid-twentieth century, especially in the period between the two world wars and the thirty years after World War II. This era of rising equality was most noteworthy in the United States and has now dramatically reversed itself. It is hard to reject the conclusion that what Piketty calls "the forces of divergence"—that create rising inequality—are almost always stronger than the "forces of convergence" that create more equality.[15] Marx would certainly agree. Interestingly, when we look at the two Marxisms and the two Pikettys, there are intriguing comparisons, since the Scientific Marxists have been certain the forces of divergence would triumph but the Critical Marxists have thought it contingent and uncertain, a conclusion that both Pikettys embrace.

Piketty's signature finding—capitalism breeds high inequality almost everywhere almost all the time—is largely descriptive. It carries power and is a huge component explaining the "Piketty phenomenon" for two reasons. First, it is based on such a vast set of several centuries of data, virtually unprecedented in its historical scale, that it is a methodological tour de force. The force of the data does not make it infallible; in fact, a growing number of economists have begun to challenge aspects of it.[16] Nonetheless, the volume, meticulousness, and historical scale of the data give considerable power to the argument. When conservative critics tried to debunk the data, as in the case of Chris Giles, the chief economics editor of the British *Financial Times,* their own criticism was debunked.[17] Piketty does not just collect a lot of data; he is very transparent and very meticulous in his handling of it—and all of it is now online for anyone to examine.

Second, the finding of perpetual extreme inequality itself is so profoundly distressing—and so deeply challenging to the reigning economic consensus—that no serious intellectual, or ordinary citizen, can ignore it. For whatever the theoretical lens one is using, it leads to hard questions about capitalism that, until Piketty, have been dismissed as remnants of outdated nineteenth-century capitalist critiques. In fact, because the discovery of perpetual vast inequality brings back the ghost of Marx, it creates a potentially transformative debate about the sustainability and morality of capitalism. Nobody expected the return of Marx through the rigorous data of a Keynesian economist, but the world always surprises us. Piketty does not embrace Marx but cannot entirely reject him—and no conversation after Piketty can reasonably leave Marx entirely out of the picture.

Piketty notes that since the national income studies of the influential American economist Simon Kuznets in the mid-twentieth century, most neoclassical economists have embraced the happy, very non-Marxist, idea that the forces of convergence will triumph and a rising tide will lift all boats.[18] Piketty's book is a sensation partly because the Kuznets consensus is so central to modern economics as well as to the American embrace of capitalism. When Piketty, who admires Kuznets, ends up rejecting Kuznets's conclusion, he throws the modern world into chaos. Piketty argues that Kuznets did not have access to the data he needed and that his findings reflected Kuznets's immersion in mid-twentieth-century capitalist exceptionalism, where the forces of convergence were unusually strong, and those of divergence unusually weak.[19]

Piketty's explanation of his dismal findings—the nearly perpetual triumph of divergence and thus the likelihood of perpetual growing inequality—rests on the now famous "equation" $r > g$, in which r is the return on capital and g is the rate of growth of the economy or national income. $R > g$ is Piketty's economic equivalent (on a more modest scale) of Einstein's $e = mc^2$, a law so fundamental to the operation of capitalist systems that we cannot do without it.[20] In its apparent scientific or mathematical framing, it more reflects Piketty 1 than Piketty 2, who might be less enthused about the scientific pretense or framing but who does not reject the potentially dire implications for capitalism.

Because $r > g$ has been so widely discussed, I will present it simply and concisely. Piketty's argument is that if r (the rate of return on capital, that is, the rent or dividends received from property and stocks) is greater than g (the rate of growth in the economy or in national income), inequality will logically increase. In some ways, this is less a theory than a tautology. As Piketty writes,

> When the rate of return on capital significantly exceeds the growth rate of the economy ... then it logically follows that inherited wealth grows faster than output and income. People with inherited wealth need save only a portion of their income from capital to see that capital grow more quickly than the economy as a whole. Under such conditions, it is almost inevitable that inherited wealth will dominate wealth amassed from a lifetime's labor by a wide margin, and the concentration of capital will attain extremely high levels—levels potentially incompatible with the meritocratic values and principles of social justice fundamental to democratic societies.[21]

While $r > g$ is not the same as concluding that rising inequality is inevitable, Piketty is not sanguine. He explains, "In the model I propose, divergence is not perpetual and is only one of several possible future directions for the distribution of wealth. But the possibilities are not heartening."[22]

The disheartening prospects are rooted in history—and in the data that Piketty presents. Over several centuries and across more than twenty countries, Piketty finds that the rate of return on capital hovers around 4 to 5 percent. But the rate of economic growth over this same historical expanse and across the same countries hovers around 1 percent or slightly above. Moreover, this disparity remains true in the early twenty-first century, where high technology, population growth, and rising education and skill would all seem to lift the rate of growth above the return to capital. This leads, as we shall see later, to Piketty puncturing very important myths about technology, skill, and growth, and will send more economists and capitalist proponents racing to their doctor or pharmacy for more antidepressants.

Piketty's other observations on $r > g$ are even more telling—and should strike terror in those who have committed to capitalism and market economics. The rather dire prospects for ever-growing inequality—and the reality of $r > g$—is not, he emphasizes, a sign of market imperfections or a flaw in capitalism but of its inherent logic. Piketty writes: "Specifically it is important to note that the fundamental $r > g$ inequality has nothing to do with market imperfection. Quite the contrary: the more perfect the capital market (in the economist's sense), the more likely r is to be greater than g."[23]

Translation: the more perfectly the market is operating according to neoclassical economic theory and capitalist logic, the more likely one is to see widening inequality. Extreme inequality is not a sign of imperfect, flawed, or badly working capitalist markets. It is a sign of capitalist markets operating precisely as they are intended to function, precisely as they are wired. This means a perfectly functioning capitalist market has no inherent deterrent to ever-expanding inequality and has very strong forces promoting it. The possible conclusion is that potentially destabilizing and unjust inequality is nearly baked into the DNA of capitalism, something that Piketty ultimately rejects as an iron law, but only with reliance on some political utopianism.

Yet there are at least two important criticisms of Piketty's $r > g$. If we ask why the rate of return on capital tends to exceed the rate of growth (or why is $r > g$), Piketty offers no theory at all. A number of critics, such as the Marxist David Harvey and Keynesian economist James Galbraith, have made this point forcefully, and it undermines the idea that Piketty has offered a new "grand theory" of capitalism or of inequality. It is, instead, a descriptive analysis, based on the historical data he has collected.[24] Harvey observes that $r > g$, which Piketty presents as a "central contradiction" of capital, is a "statistical regularity that hardly constitutes an adequate explanation, let alone a law. So what forces produce and sustain such a contradiction? Piketty does not say. The law is the law and that is that. Marx would obviously have attributed the existence of such a law to the imbalance of power between capital and labor. And that explanation still holds water."[25] Harvey, probably the most influential Marxist writer in the world today, thereby dismisses the idea that Piketty has any theory at all; rather, it is a statistical observation that one has to turn to Marx to explain. Harvey is not so much rejecting Piketty's findings as saying that they can be only understood through a Marxist framework.

To compound the problem, the data are subject to question because of their concept and measurement of wealth or capital, as discussed earlier. Piketty, to repeat, defines capital not just as the physical stock of production integral to production, as Marx did, but also personal property unrelated to production as well as financial assets, such as stocks, bonds, and derivatives, which are so subject to speculative bubbles and financial madness in the markets that they offer no stable or valid way of assessing real wealth, a point made by both Harvey and Galbraith that I discussed earlier. If his measurement of capital is flawed, then so is r—or the return on capital—and we cannot be assured that his historical data at the heart of the book are reliable.

Of course, all definitions of capital have problems, since they inevitably involve market valuations that are not true measures of utility and are always subject to fluctuation. This is true of the physical stock of productive capital—land, tools, and machines—as well. And if we move toward what Marx called "use value" to measure wealth instead of "exchange value" (the value priced on the market), we get into other problems of subjective judgment. So Piketty's data on capital may be highly vulnerable to critique because of the way he defines capital, but this is true of virtually any definition, including concepts of capital that only involve the physical stock involved in production.

At minimum, despite these contentious problems, Piketty has resurrected a new conversation about capitalism that challenges the invisible hand theory that goes back three centuries to Adam Smith. The forces of divergence may not be inevitable, but it takes major political intervention in the economy to prevent them from taking precedence. And these precedents have largely failed in almost all periods of capitalist history, leading to the perpetual extreme capitalist inequality that is the story of Piketty's data.

Is Piketty thereby reintroducing Marx as a crucial voice in the twenty-first century? No, and yes. No—because Piketty's reasoning is not based on a view of class exploitation in which the capitalist class is pursuing a clear agenda to immiserate workers and maximize inequality. Remember that Piketty's class is not Marx's class, and that it is based solely on position in the hierarchy of inequality rather than domination of workers in production. Piketty's class analysis almost reverses Marx's causation. Marx argues that capitalist classes socially and politically organize to create inequality—raising their income and profits through exploitatively extracting income or wealth of those beneath them by seizing control of the means of production. Piketty, in contrast, argues that inequality itself gives rise to unequal classes, each of which may pursue further capital accumulation for themselves but are not necessarily inherently antagonistic or exploitative toward statistical groupings on the hierarchy beneath them. Piketty 1 might very well deny any inherent concept of exploitation at all in his conception of classes. This, however, is not the whole story. When I asked Piketty whether his classes have "class interests" and whether they lead to class conflict, his answer was clearly yes: "My 'classes' are continuous and multidimensional, but of course they do have class interests and generate class conflict."[26]

This is the voice of Piketty 2, who is ready to acknowledge that the 1% and others at the very top may organize to push those on the hierarchy lower down. He is clear that top managers unfairly set their own extremely high salaries. But while there is class conflict, exploitation is by no means baked centrally into his definition of the 1% or any other class, and all Piketty classes—no matter how high up—may seek to accumulate without any intent to exploit—and perhaps sometimes without exploiting.

This represents serious differences with Marx but does not end the conversation with him. There is enough commentary by Piketty 2 about the use and abuse of power in the markets—and about the capitalist market as inherently a social and political construction—that it becomes illogical to dismiss the Marxist view. Even Piketty 1 leans toward the idea that the 1% are using political muscle to dictate their own salaries, and, like Marx, rejects the idea that top executives are paid on the basis of their productivity rather than their ability to self-deal.[27]

Here is the beginning of a very qualified or limited "yes to Marx"—that Piketty is reviving, if inadvertently. But before turning completely to the yes, let us, to be fair, highlight more of the "no." Piketty 1—and often Piketty 2—uses a mode of analysis that is like Marx mainly in its commitment to a historical approach, something very important given most economists' rejection of history. Check your own economics department where you go or went to school, and see how many economic historians are there. But beyond this crucial similarity, the logic and categories of analysis are centrally different. Marx is intently focused on capitalist class strategies to reduce wages, extend unpaid hours, and otherwise repress or abuse the workers, using both their own power in the workplace and political power they cultivate in the state to enhance their own profit at the expense of worker well-being.[28]

One of the greatest differences with Marx is Piketty's failure to examine closely the role of the 1% in capturing the state and harnessing it to its own interests. There is a noteworthy lack of attention, as I elaborated in the previous chapter on politics, to class-based political transformations in the United States, especially the New Deal and, later, the Reagan revolution. Neo-Marxists and even many American Keynesians put a central spotlight on state policy and how the 1% or capitalist class relies overwhelmingly on state initiatives, with enormous success in periods such as the Reagan era and beyond, to advance their own interests, repress the 99%, and do enormous harm to the society and natural environment. The fact that the Reagan revolution was central to creating rising inequality again today makes Piketty's failure to discuss it in any depth not just a departure from neo-Marxism but a broader problem in his political analysis. The same failure is evident in Piketty's limited discussion of the New Deal, another important omission since it helps to explain the uniquely egalitarian trend during the mid-twentieth century, and because it reflected the way the working class can organize and shape state policy benefiting its own class interests.

While Piketty 2, nonetheless, speaks frequently about the importance of social and political dynamics, it is less emphasized by Piketty 1, who has the stronger voice in the book. Piketty analyzes capitalist inequality less through the lens of class or social exploitation than through the examination of capital accumulation and abstracted and "impersonal" mechanics of economic systems, whether of supply-and-demand dynamics or of factors involving population growth, technological change, economic growth rates, saving rates, and other concepts associated with conventional economics. $R > g$ is not an equation about social exploitation but about the impersonal dynamics of accumulation, a set of laws or arrangements that work "on their own steam," more or less the way a steam engine works. It doesn't require human intent and is not driven by the aims of dehumanization and dispossession that is at the center of Marx's account of capitalism and inequality.

This argument, though, requires one further set of qualifications. Scientific Marxists also looked for impersonal laws of capitalism that worked almost independently of human intent. Scientific Marxists have some relation to Piketty, especially Piketty 1. Even though the analysis is different, both are operating at the structural level that sometimes appears to filter out human agency of any kind. Both Scientific Marxists and Piketty 1 are looking for some kind of universal capitalist laws that have considerable, though far from complete, autonomy from human beings and their social and political environment.[29]

This takes us, finally, to the question of the inevitability of inequality in capitalism—and the implications for capitalism's future. Here again, there is a "yes" and a "no" about whether Piketty is re-evoking Marx. The "no to Marx" is that Piketty is very clear that he views Marx as apocalyptic, since Marx ties growing class inequality to capitalist collapse. Piketty explicitly rejects this, even when he talks about the dismal prospects of the forces of convergence winning over the forces of divergence. Marx, or at least Scientific Marxists, would see Piketty as naive; the forces of divergence—or inequality—are inevitably dominant in capitalism, so much so that they will inexorably lead to capitalist self-destruction, through collapse or revolution.

Piketty commits to a discourse of "contingency," meaning that it is impossible to know whether the forces of divergence or inequality will triumph over those of convergence, since the outcome is not pre-determined. He argues that capitalism contains "powerful forces pushing toward divergence, or at any rate toward an extremely high level of inequality. Forces of convergence also exist, and in certain countries at certain times, they may prevail, but the forces of divergence can at any point regain the upper hand, as seems to be happening now at the beginning of the twenty-first century."[30]

Why is there contingency? First, because it is impossible to predict with any great confidence the strength of the impersonal mechanistic economic forces, such as technology, population growth, changing age structures, rates of investment and interest, and other structural forces that affect the balance of r and g. Second, because it is even more difficult to predict the evolution of social and political forces—such as the role of government and social movements—that can decisively alter the relation between r and g.

In any case, Piketty rejects any iron law of the inevitability of extreme capitalist inequality. This is important—and more than a little heretical—because mainstream economists, who aspire to be physicists, believe in impersonal iron laws shaping the operation of markets. Iron laws do not permit contingency, bespeaking instead inevitability. From Adam Smith to David Ricardo to Simon Kuznets to Milton Friedman, their conclusion is that convergence will trump divergence—that is, that a fair system of relative equality will prevail. Piketty does not say they are always wrong, but he says that they are *often* wrong—and that there is no inevitability—either toward the sunny outcome of the professional economists or the apocalypse of the Scientific Marxist.

The contingent Piketty is more the voice of Piketty 2, who emphasizes that economics can never be physics and there are no invariant or iron laws across all societies because the market reflects social values and politics that differ from society to society and profoundly affect the operation of the economy. So contingency—the uncertainty about whether inequality or equality forces will prevail—is the only certainty, since social and political forces of human agency that cannot be predicted will decisively affect the outcomes of the market. In this respect, Piketty 2 is echoing the Critical Marxists who argued against the Scientific Marxists that there is no inevitability because everything in capitalism ultimately depends on social and political struggles whose outcome cannot be known. Human agency—or politics—cannot be reduced to a scientific formula, a conclusion that the Scientific Marxists would dispute, as they are certain that structural forces guarantee capitalist collapse.

Discussion Questions

1. What facts about inequality disturb you? Does extreme inequality seem unjust to you or is it a sign of a healthy economy?
2. Does the long history of inequality convince you that capitalism dooms us to extreme inequality?
3. How does Piketty explain the rise and grip of extreme inequality?
4. How does Piketty's interpretation differ from Marx's?
5. Will extreme inequality destabilize America, creating deep economic or political crises?
6. What do you see as the solution to inequality?
7. Can more and freer higher education for all solve the problem?
8. If not, what are the other possible solutions, or do you feel there are no answers?

8

♦ ♦ ♦

THE DEATH OF MERITOCRACY

Is America a meritocracy? Does the 1% earn its money, or inherit it? Do the poor and working classes deserve their low wages and poverty? If not, are they exploited, and is this inherent in capitalism? How much do power and social mores determine wages of lower-income people? Does the remarkable size of inherited wealth undermine any conception of America or capitalism as a meritocratic system? Is there enough meritocracy in America to justify the inequality between the 1% and the 99%—and to justify capitalism itself?

Piketty has started yet another conversation—about whether our economy is truly a meritocracy. The question about meritocracy is not just academic—it lies at the heart of America's conception of itself. The consensus of economists and most Americans has been that the United States is an exceptional nation because it believes in merit and has created a capitalist system that allows it to flourish. When you start to question this assumption—and there is plenty of ammunition in Piketty to do so—you shake the foundations of our national pride and our belief in the morality of capitalism.

Economists do not like to get into moral debates, seeing themselves practicing a science that doesn't rest on social or political values.[1] But the mainstream economic consensus embracing capitalism rests on the idea that capitalism is meritocratic, and that this has been scientifically demonstrated.[2] Piketty, however, argues that much of conventional economics and market theory is nothing more than "ideology," that functions to justify the inequalities of the system. At the heart of that ideology is the consensus on meritocracy.[3]

Meritocratic ideology goes back to the Puritans who sailed over the ocean to America four hundred years ago. Success in the market reflected God's grace—and thus personal merit or being a worthy person—while failure was a sure sign of sin or being a worthless soul. The intensity of this belief helped lead the sociologist Max Weber to the idea that the Protestant ethic gave rise to capitalism, because it motivated people to succeed in the market and gave the "winners" a divine legitimation of the right to their spoils.[4] Capitalism gave economically ambitious people assurance that God ordained their worldly success, while reducing any guilt about the suffering of the losers.

Meritocracy still reigns in the moral debate about the economy today. Capitalism, as Piketty dramatically shows, produces vast gaps between the winners and losers, gaps so large that they raise the question of whether anything can justify them. But we have a modern-day Puritanism that continues to validate the winners as "makers" and the losers as "takers." Vice President Republican candidate Paul Ryan said in 2012 that welfare was actually an "injustice to the poor" because it made them lazy "takers" unwilling to work.[5] These sentiments, voiced by both Ryan and his presidential running mate, Mitt Romney, during their campaigns, did not propel them to victory but nonetheless resonated with a very large number of people, including many religious Americans who follow the "gospel of prosperity" preached by televangelists like Joel Osteen, Kenneth Copeland, Benny Hinn, and Pat Robertson. The prosperity gospel preaches that "televangelists use their own interpretation of Christian scripture on giving and charity ... to convince their followers that poverty is caused by not believing that wealth is good and a natural spiritual state of being a true Christian. The richer you are as a Christian the more you are closer to God and his favor."[6] Capitalism is the perfect system for a godly people, whose god wants them to work hard and make lots of money.

Throughout our society, the view that capitalism rewards hard work, talent, and merit while punishing those who are lazy, dependent, or lacking skill remains the central moral premise sustaining our capitalist order. The idea of capitalist meritocracy is the heart of the Republican Party ideology; it is also largely embraced by the Democratic Party leadership; and it resonates very strongly with the views of the capitalist class. It has "trickled down" to a very sizable percentage of the US population, who view American society as rewarding virtuous winners and punishing worthless losers.[7]

Piketty has opened a new conversation about capitalist meritocracy and morality. Part of it flows simply from the size of the inequality he documents; are the 1% possibly that much better or meritorious than all the rest of us? Piketty often thinks like a mainstream economist, but he, especially Piketty 2, seems to want the rest of us to think like moralists as he writes about inequality and other aspects of capitalism. At least four themes, central to Piketty's work, raise uncomfortable challenges to the idea of capitalist meritocracy.

One is the idea of patrimonial capitalism and the importance of inherited wealth and caste in our economy. The second is his challenge to productivity theory that equates wages with the merit of workers' contribution. The third is his challenge to mechanistic economics that denies the importance of social and political power shaping the rules and success of the upper classes. And the fourth returns to the question of the size and future of inequality—and whether any degree of merit can justify such huge, destructive divisions in the population.

Consider first the idea of patrimonial capitalism, the key concept in Piketty's book and arguably the one most threatening to the concept of American meritocracy. Patrimonial capitalist societies are usually associated with Belle Époque Europe and the dynastic worlds of wealth written about by the nineteenth-century great novelists, particularly Balzac and Austen, as well as the Gilded Age capitalism of America in the late nineteenth century.[8] They bring up images of vast landed estates run by the gentry, as well as new industrial aristocrats seeking to imitate the nobility of the late Middle Ages and early Renaissance. In the United States, Gilded Age tycoons such as Vanderbilt and Rockefeller built summer cottages that resembled the castles of the European nobility. The defining quality of all these societies—where capitalist elites aped medieval nobility—was the central role of inherited wealth. Inheritance played a far more important role than work or earned income from labor in early patrimonial capitalism, a caste system in which inherited wealth in dynastic families ruled the roost. Piketty's work, which returns repeatedly to the literary work of Balzac and Austen, is most original in its pointing to inheritance and the caste principle as not just the past of capitalism but very likely its future, with inherited wealth arguably destined to play an even greater role in twenty-first-century American patrimonial capitalism than in Old Europe.

What could be more threating to concepts of meritocracy than the return of vast inherited wealth? Inheritance may reflect merit of one's parents, but it tells us nothing about our own merit. If fortune and the good life are largely derived from the wealth of our parents rather than our own efforts, the entire concept of meritocracy is undermined. If rich people live off of inherited wealth, as the children of dynastic families in Belle Époque Europe or of the Rockefellers or Morgans in the United States did, the principle of meritocracy is lost, and we return to the caste morality of the feudal ages, where the wealthy may play and never do a day's work. If you had to work in feudal times, as noted in Chapter 5, that was a sign that you were of inferior blood, of a lower "essence." Inheritance and meritocracy are incompatible and contradictory moral principles.

People living from inherited wealth are "rentiers," historically living off of rent from their landed estates—and today off returns from their stocks and bonds. Today's 1% is both a rentier class and salaried elite, claiming that they have proven their worth through their enormous contribution to the value of the firm.[9] In fact, they tend to live off income from capital or inherited wealth—and their children can live entirely from their inheritances.

Inheritance returns us to the concept of caste, a precapitalist idea central in medieval feudalism, completely at odds with the capitalist ideology of meritocracy. Castes gain privilege not through the proved merit of their work but via their blood or inherited wealth. As classes take on more the character of castes, the class conversation will be deeply transformed, because privileged caste classes derive their privilege from feudal rather than capitalist principles.

The future, says Piketty, will likely be marked by unbelievably large inherited fortunes. At a certain threshold, he argues, massive fortunes "grow at extremely high rates, regardless of whether the owner of the fortune works or not."[10] He points out that Bill Gates's wealth while he worked at Microsoft between 1990 and 2010 did not grow faster than that of Liliane Bettencourt, the heiress of L'Oreal, a perfume and cosmetics dynasty, who never worked a day in her life but whose fortune grew from $2 billion in 1990 to $25 billion in 2010. Piketty also points out that Steve Jobs, who could make serious meritocratic claims, was much poorer than "dozens of people with inherited fortunes larger than Jobs'. Obviously wealth is not just a matter of merit. The reason for this is simply that the return on inherited fortunes is often very high solely because of their initial size."[11] The bottom line: as society is organized increasingly of, by, and for the patrimonial dynastic families, with their wealth and power based on inheritance in a caste order, meritocracy will no longer be our reality. The arguments since the Puritans that legitimated capitalist wealth on the basis of hard work will be buried under the medieval caste morality of inheritance. And the very morality of capitalism—always organized around the ideal of hard work and rewards for the most talented—will almost certainly erode, even though high earners will use marketers, teachers, and preachers to sustain it to justify their fortunes.

Second, Piketty is challenging meritocracy by his critique of the theory of marginal productivity as the source of income inequality. Earlier, we discussed Piketty's argument that while top executives claim that their multimillion-dollar salary payments are based on their extraordinary contribution to the firm, this is demonstrably bogus. One cannot measure their productivity, and the super-managers set their own huge salaries through "self-dealing." Piketty opens up a new conversation about meritocracy by showing that the mainstream economic theory of marginal productivity is pure "ideology" when applied to executive 1% salaries, an effort by the 1% itself (and the economists who provide the rich ammunition) to morally legitimate their astronomical compensation on the basis of exceptional merit.[12] Piketty calls this "meritocratic extremism," where, especially in the United States, people seem to need "to designate certain individuals as 'winners' and to reward them all the more generously if they seem to be selected on the basis of their intrinsic merits rather than birth or background."[13] But Piketty points out that the extravagance of the 1% salaries and corporate executives' power in shaping their own compensation is demonstrably eroding the credibility of the United States as a meritocracy. The idea of extreme marginal productivity justifying extreme salaries for the super-managers "becomes something close to a pure ideological construct on the basis of which a justification for higher status can be elaborated."[14]

When it comes to the income of the rest of the labor force, Piketty is less ready to throw out the meritocratic argument, although he doesn't completely endorse it and opens another important conversation. In contrast to top executives, Piketty believes that marginal productivity has more credibility in explaining both the low wages of the bottom 50 percent and the moderate salaries of the next 40 percent. For the bottom half of the population, Piketty argues that jobs are relatively uniform and deskilled. "When a job is replicable, as in the case of an assembly-line worker or fast-food server, we can give an approximate estimate of the 'marginal product' that would be realized by adding one additional worker or waiter."[15] If we can measure productivity, then one can make a plausible case, he argues, that wages are reflecting marginal productivity and thus reflect merit.

But even here, Piketty—and this is more Piketty 2—argues that with the waiter or fast-food server, estimates of marginal productivity can be made only "with a considerable margin of error."[16] So even in the most favorable circumstances, the productivity of the worker can be known only vaguely and is only one very imperfect factor among others shaping wages. Piketty 2 goes into great detail, as noted earlier, about the entire labor market as a social construction, a set of social arrangements based on values and customs and privilege, with wages partially determined by bargaining power rather than productivity. This argument, which begins to evoke Marx's view of the labor market as less an impersonal supply-and-demand market than an exploitative power game, pops up just enough in Piketty to open a new conversation about the strength of meritocratic forces even with jobs whose productivity might be able to be estimated with at least a modest degree of accuracy.

Even Piketty 2 doesn't go far enough in this discussion, and the new conversation should take us further into the discussion of power. Piketty largely ignores the broad corporate strategy of transforming jobs from full-time work with solid benefits to contingent work with no benefits, a strategy politically backed by the Reagan revolution and fulfilled by destruction of unions, global outsourcing, replacing workers with robots and other technology, and attacks on government social welfare and entitlement programs.[17] Is the paltry wage of the adjunct professors—who together are now 70 percent of all university professors—a reflection of their low productivity and merit, or is it the clear outcome of an empowered and corporatized university administration using its power to force down professors' salaries? No sane person who knows the university well would argue that the new generation of adjunct professors is so poorly paid now because it is so less productive or talented than earlier tenured professor generations with much higher salaries. This is clearly a case of shifts in political power and corporate restructuring of the academic labor market—and is a rather graphic demonstration of how absurd meritocratic arguments are in explaining or justifying adjunct faculty salaries that are so low as to be beneath living wages.

The adjunct professor case takes us to consider the middle and upper-middle class as well as the poor and working lower half of the population. The considerations of the adjunct apply to the nursing home aides and to fast-food workers, emblematic of the disinherited majority whose miserable salaries and working conditions reflect powerlessness rather than lack of skill or merit, a theme we take up shortly using nursing home workers as examples. But, more surprisingly, they also apply to a wide range of office and even professional employees. Piketty would acknowledge that the less routinized or "replicable" work of white-collar employees would make it harder to measure their productivity. And as the labor income of even these higher groups such as teachers, social workers, and government clerical and professional employees (below the top 10 percent) has slowed if not stagnated, it is almost certainly largely because of the broader corporate and political strategies described above—union-busting, outsourcing, elimination of government social welfare and pension policies—rather than declining productivity. In fact, there is evidence that labor productivity has increased, even as the national share of income represented by return on labor or wages compared to return on capital has dramatically declined.[18] This seems entirely contradictory to the logic of meritocracy, reflecting instead large shifts in the balance of power between the 1% and almost all other workers. Piketty has failed to make this case with the depth and force it deserves, and the new conversation after him should fill in this huge gap that he has left for the rest of us to analyze.

This leads to Piketty's third new challenge to the myth of capitalist meritocracy. Across the board, the economic or market assessment of worth is determined by social mores and values, typically shaped most by the wealthiest and most powerful. Piketty 2 fully acknowledges the role of social customs in governing views of the value and merit of jobs and skills, especially in regard to the work of top corporate executives.[19] "It is very difficult," he says, "for any individual firm to go against the prevailing social norms of the country in which it operates," referring to the fact that social values and norms shape views of the worth and productivity of different kinds of work. "These social norms reflect beliefs about the contributions that different individuals make to the firm's output and to economic growth in general."[20]

And Piketty 2 says that such social judgments operate to some degree at all levels of the economy, shaping the market's pricing of all work and products, quite independent of worker productivity or the true value of products. Piketty 2's argument, that social values shape perceptions of economic value—and inevitably reflect the power of the 1% in establishing social norms and perceptions—pokes deep holes in the theory of meritocracy.

A case in point is nursing aides or caretakers in nursing homes. These workers are paid minimum wage, justified by the idea that their skills and productivity are extremely low. But, since such caretakers are often women and people of color, discriminatory cultural and social norms shape the view of both the value and skill of such work. Anyone whose parents have gone into a nursing home knows that such social valuations are inhuman and often entirely at odds with the reality. Nursing home care is among the most challenging work in America, and it is highly valuable work. The minimal wage paid to these workers is clearly shaped by the prejudicial social judgments about these workers and their relative political powerlessness; it contradicts any rational judgment about the value of the work or the skills it demands. Piketty 2 hints at the importance of this line of argument in an extensive discussion of minimum-wage laws and the role of bargaining power in wage decisions.[21] But the conversation we need would go far deeper into this line of thinking, not just for caretaking work but for all work and workers in the economy, and it would almost certainly undermine productivity theory and meritocratic ideology far more than Piketty himself does.

Piketty's view of meritocracy as more ideology than reality is exceedingly important. His data are very persuasive about our return to an inheritance mode with some resemblance to the feudal ages and to the patrimonial systems of Belle Époque Europe, where inherited wealth also dominated. But our world today is cruel in its own way because it drapes high fortune in the morally soothing language of hard work and merit, something that the feudal era never did. In feudalism, the accepted wisdom was that the aristocrats were born into their station with a divine essence justifying their privilege. The nobility—especially in feudalism—did not claim they earned high standing through meritorious hard work. In fact, as noted in Chapter 5, their "blue blood" caste meant it was demeaning for them to work at all; God had ordained a life of leisure for them. On the other hand, the 99% caste—the disinherited majority—were born without God's grace and were condemned for their entire lives to live poor no matter how hardworking. True, they were seen as inferior and of little worth, so in some sense the victims—the 99%—were blamed both then and now, but obligations of birth in the feudal caste order meant that the lords owed protection to the serfs. What is different is that with today's meritocratic ideology, the rich are able to claim that they have earned through hard work and merit all their extraordinary wealth, removing their obligation to serve and protect the poor. Meritocracy, as Piketty argues, is an extraordinarily powerful legitimating ideology, masking the injustices of inherited wealth and a revived caste system.

Piketty opens a powerful conversation about meritocracy but just cracks open the door a bit. He is too locked into the very economics that he critiques, and too unschooled in the sociological and political analysis that he argues is essential. In the end, his arguments about extreme inequality in a rising patrimonial capitalism have the potential to blow apart the meritocratic ideology and the denial of economic caste that has morally legitimated capitalism and warded off large-scale social transformation. It is up to the rest of us to open the door wider and take us to the space that Piketty has peeked into but not fully entered.

Discussion Questions

1. Do most workers deserve the pay they get? Why or why not?
2. Are the highest-paid people in America those who work hardest or have the most talent?
3. Is meritocracy more an ideology than a reality at this point in America?
4. Why do most Americans continue to believe that we are a country based on meritocracy?
5. If patrimonial capitalism is a caste system, can it ever be a system based on work or on merit?
6. Is capitalism ever based on meritocratic principles? Can it be?
7. Is there a way to make America move closer to its own meritocratic ideals?

9

♦ ♦ ♦

THE FUTURE OF THE
AMERICAN DREAM

Is America still the land of the American Dream? Was it ever? Why is social mobility lower in the United States than in many countries of Europe? How does this relate to education and inequality? Don't education and technology promote mobility? Is inherited wealth subverting opportunity and the American Dream? Is American capitalism compatible with the American Dream?

A liberal friend told me that he didn't think most Americans cared that much about inequality. What they care about is whether they can get ahead through work, and whether their children will do better than they have. In other words, the issue is opportunity for the masses, rather than inequality across the entire population.

His view is more true of Republicans than Democrats. Americans of both parties are aware of high and rising inequality in the United States and do not like it, with 69 percent saying the government should do "a lot" or "something about it."[1] Over 90 percent of Democrats say this, against 45 percent of Republicans.[2] But virtually all groups do seem to agree that opportunity to move up is very important, hardly a surprise since this is the heart of the American Dream.

A key question, then, is whether Piketty is starting a new conversation not only about inequality but about opportunity and the American Dream. Does his work offer insights about whether opportunity is stagnating or declining as inequality increases? Is American idealism oriented toward equality of results as well as of opportunity? Is there a new conversation to be had about the future of the American Dream?

Piketty's data shed less explicit light on this question than on earlier issues discussed. He does not present much data on mobility, nor does he discuss it in any depth. But he still provides fodder for an important new debate about the American Dream. This is both because inequality is related to mobility and because Piketty makes arguments about education and skill, as well as technology, that bear not just on inequality but on opportunity. Moreover, his focus on inherited wealth and caste, productivity, and meritocracy in the book has important implications for the American Dream in the twenty-first century.

Before looking at these arguments, start with the mobility facts. They do not support the American exceptionalist view that the United States is the unique "land of opportunity," where anybody who works hard can move up and make a better life. To the contrary. The consensus that has emerged in recent years, both among scholars and politicians of both main parties, is that social mobility is lower in the United States than in Canada and most western and northern European countries. A review of more than fifty studies of nine countries found social mobility highest in Canada, Norway, Finland, and Denmark, and lowest in the United States and Britain. Sweden, Germany, and France were in the middle.[3] This has become part of Democratic boilerplate rhetoric, with President Barack Obama talking about the decline of "ladders of opportunity" and liberal economist Isabel Sawhill of the Brookings Institute saying that "it's becoming conventional wisdom that the US does not have as much mobility as other advanced countries."[4] On the conservative side, a former aide to President George W. Bush, John Bridgeland, was "shocked" by the international rankings, saying "Republicans will not feel compelled to talk about income inequality. But they will feel a need to talk about a lack of mobility."[5] Republican politicians such as former GOP senator Rick Santorum said movement "up into the middle is actually greater, the mobility in Europe, than it is in America"; the *National Review,* an influential conservative magazine, wrote that "most Western Europe and English-speaking nations have higher rates of mobility (than the United States)"; and Paul Ryan, Mitt Romney's vice-presidential running mate in 2012, wrote that "mobility from the very bottom up" is "where the United States lags behind."[6] Piketty himself writes that "these findings stand in sharp contrast to the belief in 'American exceptionalism' that once dominated US sociology, according to which social mobility in the United States was exceptionally high compared with the class-bound societies of Europe. . . . Throughout most of the twentieth century, however, and still today, the available data suggest that social mobility has been and remains lower in the United States than in Europe."[7]

No studies have shown that the United States is turning this around. A 2014 study led by economist Emmanuel Saez, a close colleague of Piketty, but published after Piketty's book, did challenge the idea that opportunity in the United States has been falling in the past few decades, presenting controversial new findings, showing little change in US mobility during that period. That, however, did not create a sunny new picture. Saez and his colleagues confirm that the United States has long had lower mobility than many developed countries, meaning that it has not been the land of opportunity for a long period, and they do not suggest any reversal in this trend.[8]

Despite the broad consensus about this reality, it has not provoked the urgent new conversation it deserves. Piketty's work may help because his data and ideas about rising inequality help to explain the facts, and could catalyze the debate we need.

Piketty explicitly argues that high inequality tends to lead to low social mobility, a finding supported in the Saez study. This is not immediately obvious, nor is it an iron law in all places, but a little reflection makes it intuitively sensible. In a society such as Denmark, which is one of the most equal nations, it takes only small increases in income to move up from a lower class to a higher class. But in a country such as the United States, where the chasm between classes is huge, it is clear that it takes big increases in one's income to leap into a higher class. For a factory or clerical employee in the working class to become a multimillionaire (and get into the upper decile class or the top 1% class) is obviously nearly impossible—how could wages increase over his or her life to that degree? You'd have to win the lottery. For an American to move from the lower half into even the upper quartile would also take a very large increase in income that is also highly improbable, and Piketty cites data, confirmed by many studies, showing that such large lifetime increases in income are very uncommon in the United States.[9] In Denmark, though, because class incomes are so compressed, far more modest increases in income can catapult a worker into a higher class position. In relatively egalitarian societies, you don't have to win the lottery or magically inherit a fortune to move up.

To put it simply, the steeper the inequality hierarchy, the bigger the rise in wages or income it takes to move into a higher class. This does not bode well, in Piketty's analysis, for opportunity in twenty-first-century America, where wages are stagnant for most workers, and inequality, already steep, seems destined to become steeper.

Piketty offers new insights into three areas crucial to the future of both inequality and opportunity: education, meritocracy, and inheritance. In all cases, his observations are extremely important but, again, only open the door to a new conversation that we need.

Education is crucial in the mind of most Americans, because it is widely seen as the most important way that an individual can move up in America. Piketty asserts that education and the diffusion of knowledge are unquestionably the most important "force of convergence" promoting equality.[10] All through his book Piketty champions more education. But his data show a counterintuitive fact. As the average level of education in the United States rose during the twentieth century, "earned income inequality did not decrease."[11] Piketty's explanation: "Qualification levels shifted upward, a high school diploma now represents what a grade school certificate used to mean, a college degree what a high school diploma used to stand for, and so on. As technologies and workplace needs changed, all wage levels increased at similar rates so that inequality did not change."[12]

But, asks Piketty, has the increase in the average level of education among Americans increased mobility? His response: "According to the available data, the answer seems to be no ... no trend toward greater mobility over the long run."[13]

How is this possible if so many Americans are getting more education, presumably the ticket to moving up? Piketty uncovers a likely reason: the costs of educational access in the United States and who can afford it. Piketty observes that "access to the most elite US universities requires the payment of extremely high tuition fees. Furthermore those fees rose sharply in the period 1990–2010, following fairly closely the increase in top US incomes, which suggests that the reduced social mobility observed in the US in the past will decline even more in the future."[14]

Piketty clarifies the argument by introducing striking data about changing educational access by social class. "Research has shown that the proportion of college degrees earned by children whose parents belong to the bottom two quartiles of the income hierarchy stagnated at 10 to 20 percent between 1970 and 2010, while it rose from 40 to 80 percent for children with parents in the top quartile. In other words, parents' income has become an almost perfect predictor of university access."[15] Put differently, access to education has become a matter of caste; only those born into higher economic stations will get higher education degrees. This contradicts entirely the conventional capitalist idea of education and opportunity, which dismisses economic caste as irrelevant to American opportunity.

Low mobility, then, particularly among those in the lower half who most need a ticket up, comes from at least two aspects of the US education system. One is that almost 90 percent of the lower half of America does not get higher education, compared to 80 percent of the upper quarter, who get college degrees. This knocks out education as a mobility ticket for half the population, the disinherited majority. Second, the increased access to education—reflected in higher average educational levels in America—is because upper-income students are almost all going to and graduating from a university, at a rate double that of their parents.

The reason for the differences, Piketty argues, is tied to the extravagant and rising costs of college. The lower half cannot afford it—and even those in the next 40 percent are going to have to settle for a lower-level university. Piketty estimates that "the average income of the parents of Harvard students is currently about $450,000."[16] Only the 1% or the 2 percent have income that can punch that ticket!

Moreover, Piketty notes that gifts to universities—coming largely from the upper classes—are concentrated in the period when their children are of college age. This suggests that parental donations may influence college admissions, something that "does not seem entirely compatible with the idea of selection based on merit."[17] Parental donors are contributing heavily to turning American higher education into a caste system.

Piketty argues that equal opportunity to higher education is critically important for mobility. But because educational costs are escalating rather than declining, lower and middle Americans may be more likely to get less rather than more education than their parents. As inequality increases, an educational system with rising costs seems like a recipe for declining mobility of the lower and middle classes. Piketty suggests that unless university costs are drastically reduced, and other social or cultural forces develop that improve prospects of admission for lower-income students, it is hard to imagine the resurrection of the American

Dream.[18] Of course, some point to the rise of online education as drastically reducing the cost of higher education, but at this stage that seems remote, as the early grand hopes for it have not been realized, and the big online universities, such as Phoenix and Trump, have run into legal problems, since they take money from students who mostly drop out and are left with steep student debts.

Piketty does not discuss here another key issue that we will bring up later. Education cannot guarantee mobility. If jobs—and good-paying ones—decline and become scarce, no amount of education will increase mobility for most of the population. This goes beyond where Piketty does, to the question of whether even a highly educated population will have upward mobility in a world where even many skilled jobs are outsourced or performed by robots.[19]

Piketty's insights about meritocracy should, along with education, be part of the new conversation we need about the future of the American Dream. Having already earlier discussed meritocracy at some length, we need consider only two additional aspects related to mobility. One, again, has to do with education. As just noted, Piketty makes clear that access to education is increasingly less tied to merit than to parental income or wealth, that is, to caste. But education is supposed to be a foundation of meritocracy in America, with the university degree presumably certifying that the graduate has demonstrated merit and can move into a job rewarding it. If the degree is instead largely reflecting the income of parents, any mobility the degree confers reflects less a meritocracy than a financial auction won by the highest bidder. In this case, the mobility that comes with higher education is at least partially bought rather than earned, and this type of mobility is less likely to be honored or to endure, because it will be rightfully seen as an unfair reward to the already privileged, a caste reward inherited from one's parents rather than something reflecting one's own intelligence or abilities.

Second, recall Piketty's critique of the theory of marginal productivity, which undermines the idea that higher incomes—especially at the top—reflect merit; instead it reflects power to set wages. If we take Piketty 2's extension of doubt about productivity as the main force, shaping not only the pay of corporate executives but the wages of much of the population, this not only undermines the American meritocracy ideal but subverts any moral model of social mobility. If it is not one's productivity that garners higher income—but rather social privilege or political power—then whatever mobility exists throughout the economy comes under a giant cloud. Those who are mobile may simply be capitalizing on privilege from their parents (the way of the caste) or clawing their way up through power instead of merit. In this case, if we get mobility, it is not the kind idealized in the American Dream. It becomes instead a sociopathic accomplishment—something like that depicted in *The Wolf of Wall Street*. Mobility, especially at the top, may survive, but it will likely be a form that appears to demean the American Dream, tending to strip it of legitimacy.[20]

This is closely tied to Piketty's third contribution to mobility, which relates to the return of patrimonial capitalism and the rising importance of inherited wealth and caste classes. Because the heart of Piketty's argument is that the United States is hurling toward a new twenty-first-century form of patrimonial capitalism, the question arises: What kind of mobility is possible within such a system, in which inherited wealth tends to gain more and more importance?

Inheritance and social mobility are contradictory and antagonistic principles. A society based entirely on inheritance would be a pure caste system, in which mobility is impossible. In the feudal societies of the Middle Ages, one was born into one's caste, and it was impossible to move up (or down) into another caste (although merchants occasionally bought noble titles and some merchants could also perform warrior feats that would raise them in the hierarchy). A society dominated by caste is one, by definition, that marginalizes or entirely eliminates mobility.

Patrimonial capitalism is less extreme, but similarly promotes inheritance and caste at the expense of mobility. Piketty's romp through the novels of Balzac and Austen shows a world in which those who work hard may see some mobility, but whatever status they eke out will pale compared to the inherited privilege of patrimonial elites. He describes the mobility of those working hard to get ahead as gaining "crumbs," compared to the inherited wealth of the dynastic families.[21]

As he looks forward into the twenty-first century, Piketty sees the return of Balzac's and Austen's world. Mobility may survive, particularly among the middle classes who gain access to higher education. But they also will gain "crumbs" compared to the inherited fortunes of the upper classes, peopled by fabulously rich corporate executives such as Bill Gates, Warren Buffet, and the Koch brothers. The children of Gates and the Kochs will inherit far more wealth than the dynastic families of Balzac and Austin's era. Children of parents who have rocketed to the top inherit their parents' new caste status. Bill Clinton may have been born much lower on the hierarchy than George W. Bush, but Chelsea Clinton is in the same caste as Barbara and Jenna Bush, W's daughters. The same is true of Obama's daughters, even though they are black.

America's new patrimonial capitalism will be organized around caste classes. Caste classes in capitalist America will permit more mobility than the medieval feudal caste order, which had almost no mobility. But caste classes are defined by their relative immobility, with members largely positioned for life in the station to which they are born.

Privileged caste classes are in a position to set the rules to decrease mobility of all those below them. This is a crucial issue of power, which is partially implicit in Piketty 2, but much clearer in a neo-Marxist vision. It raises the question that we don't talk much about today: whether the American capitalist system is compatible with the American Dream. We are seeing a contradiction inherent within capitalism, especially the patrimonial form. Capitalism claims to underpin the American Dream, but its caste character subverts the mobility that it professes.

Piketty sees no iron law that dictates with certainty how much mobility can exist within the patrimonial capitalism he now sees emerging. Piketty 1 comes closer to the idea that structural forces will largely determine the outcome, and his arguments suggest that the "forces of divergence" have sufficient potency that mobility may very likely be substantially reduced.[22] Piketty 2 sees more room for human and political agency, suggesting that if they mobilize their political will, Americans can remold patrimonial capitalism to permit a great deal more mobility, by decreasing inequality through income and wealth taxes.[23] At the least, Piketty 2 suggests that we cannot know with any certainty whether mobility will be drastically reduced in the coming century of patrimonial capitalism. In fact, at times he seems optimistic that wealth taxes and other progressive policies, associated with the European welfare state, will open up our capitalist system and revive the American Dream, a hope that is shared by many if not most Keynesians. With Piketty-type policy interventions, Keynesians see no enduring contradiction between capitalism and the American Dream.[24] If they did, they likely would have to abandon their embrace of capitalism, which would be tantamount to renouncing Keynesianism.

This, however, is a particular problem for Piketty, whose analysis of caste in patrimonial capitalism suggests limits to many traditional

Keynesian solutions. Simply decreasing inequality does not necessarily weaken the caste character of patrimonial capitalism. The 1% caste at the top is not going to be mortally wounded by higher taxes, and its members will continue to be able to impose rules leading to a system heavily based on caste principles. Piketty's revelations about patrimonial capitalism suggest caste barriers that may require solutions well beyond what Keynesians normally entertain, including beyond progressive taxation, Piketty's choice.

Fortunately, the new post-Piketty conversation of the coming century will not be shaped only by Keynesians. Among the participants at the global level will be "new economy economists," including a new generation of green, localist, "solidarity economists," or neo-Marxists with a variety of other views.[25] It will also include the voices of social movements and ordinary citizens, something that Piketty strongly endorses.

In contrast with Keynesians, neo-Marxists have a much darker view of the compatibility of capitalism with the American Dream. For the Scientific Marxists, structural forces lead toward a collapse of the capitalism system, as the overproduction of capital leads to the decline of capital productivity and the collapse of demand by workers, who are left without jobs or disposable income. As that system works its way toward collapse, the structural forces lead toward a one-way mobility for almost all the population: downward.[26]

The Scientific Marxist sees downward mobility guaranteed by the capture of government by the capitalist class. The government, structurally the handmaiden of the corporate executive class, sets the rules that restrain mobility across most of the vast working class, creating a disinherited majority constituting a lower caste. Corporate strategies to maximize short-term profit by outsourcing, deregulating, breaking unions, and increasing corporate welfare while shifting tax burdens away from the wealthy will be locked in by state policy. Austerity, defined as defunding social programs and enforcing antilabor policies, has been locked into state policy since the Reagan revolution. It creates a twenty-first-century capitalism that is increasingly incompatible with mobility and the American Dream, keeping the disinherited majority in its place as a lifelong lower caste. The capitalist state will permanently prevent the interventions imagined by Piketty 2 and the Keynesians, which in any case would be insufficient to ward off capitalist self-destruction or the caste character of patrimonial capitalism.[27]

Critical Marxists would argue, along with Piketty 2, that there is no absolute inevitability of capitalist collapse—nor of eternal caste. Agency, as noted earlier, cannot be reduced to the formulas of physics or to any iron laws of capitalism. Yet Critical Marxists would find Piketty 2's solutions—and other Keynesian policy solutions within the capitalist order—as improbable. American capitalism, for them, too, cannot be made compatible with the American Dream, largely because of the capitalist control of the state that locks in the caste class system and permanently disenfranchises the disinherited majority.[28]

But there are several other possible scenarios, highlighted not just by Critical Marxists but by other economic schools and by social movements in the United States and around the world. One, the most optimistic, is that the mass of the population—that is, the disinherited majority—driven by the myths of opportunity and the American Dream, will find patrimonial capitalism so morally at odds with their idea of America that they will reject the patrimonial system or even seek to transform capitalism itself, mobilizing to create a more open and cooperative economy promoting the public interest. A second view is that they will struggle for more modest changes that might promote more mobility in the short to medium run but will eventually run up against the internal contradictions of patrimonial capitalism—or any other capitalist model. A third is that they might turn to right-wing populism as described by Thomas Frank in *What's the Matter with Kansas.*[29] Like Piketty 2, Critical Marxists would shy away from any iron law that predicts the future with any certainty. But their view of internal class antagonisms and exploitation, increasingly taking the form of a caste system, and the control exercised by the corporate class over the state, make it very likely that we will, for a considerable period, live in an American capitalism increasingly based on caste and thus incompatible with the American Dream.

Discussion Questions

1. Do you think the American Dream is still alive today?
2. Is opportunity possible in the caste system of patrimonial capitalism described by Piketty?
3. Do you think that Americans who work hard still have a good opportunity to move up? Did they ever?

4. Is opportunity still high for poor and lower-income workers? Was it ever?

5. Is opportunity high for the middle classes? How much mobility can they expect?

6. Do you think the younger generation today will live a better life than their parents?

7. Why do you think America's social mobility is now less than in Canada and many European countries?

8. Do you think education is a route up for most Americans?

9. Do you worry that the American Dream cannot be realized in the twenty-first century? What would it take to see that happen?

10

♦ ♦ ♦

WEALTH AND WAR

What is the relation between US capitalism, inequality, and war? Relative equality came only during the period of the two world wars. Does this imply capitalism needs war to create growth and equality? Is this a form of military Keynesianism, central to propping up capitalism?

The era of the mid-twentieth century plays an important part in Piketty's analysis. This period, which centered on World Wars I and II, as well as the Great Depression, was unique. Piketty highlights it as the major period in western Europe and the United States in which inequality significantly declined and equality increased.[1]

This economic exceptionalism seems to suggest that war can be a significant factor promoting equality. Big wars appeared to promote the forces of convergence and weaken the forces of divergence. Throughout the mid-twentieth-century war and postwar period, the capital/income ratio declined both in Europe and the United States, reducing inequality. This raises the question of whether war plays a necessary function in promoting equality and sustaining capitalism.

Piketty certainly does not propose war as the solution to the crises of inequality and capitalism. But in highlighting the exceptionalism of the mid-twentieth-century period, he does identify war as one of the factors contributing to the growth of equality, both directly and indirectly. Piketty does not expand this discussion into a broader analysis of the role of war—or war spending—in Western capitalism, nor does he look at motives for war or who profits, factors that also may have a major effect on the economy and inequality and deserve an extended critical analysis, from both an economic and a moral perspective.

Like many Keynesians, Piketty is largely silent about Western militarism and imperialism, a serious omission. This silence reflects the approach of most Keynesian economists, and it is mainly neo-Marxist political economists who probe these issues in depth.[2] Many other political economists and analysts of US foreign policy, though, have reflected on the relation between war, profits, and inequality, and it is worth considering how Piketty's brief discussion changes the conversation, if at all.[3]

The effect of war has partly to do with its destruction of capital. Bombs destroy property and much of the accumulated wealth in a society. This is obvious in large-scale wars, but in Piketty's framework it has an outcome not typically discussed. Anything that destroys wealth tends to reduce the capital/income ratio, and thus has an equalizing effect.[4]

In France and Britain during World War II, this direct effect of physical destruction was significant, obviously more so than in the United States, where war did not destroy the homeland. However, even in Europe physical destruction was not the most important factor; "the budgetary and political shocks of two wars proved far more destructive to capital than combat itself."[5] Piketty highlights several non-combat-related factors very important in Europe: the collapse of foreign assets due to foreign revolutions and decolonization as well as very low saving rates that led the wealthy to sell off their assets, partly as a strategy to maintain their standard of living.[6] Other related factors, only partly related to war, such as the German economic crisis caused partly by the harsh settlement of World War I, and subsequently the global Great Depression, also wiped out much capital. Between 1913 and 1950 the decline in the capital/income ratio was so high that it represented "the euthanasia of the European capitalists."[7]

All these war-related "shocks" destroyed much of the European economy but disproportionately destroyed wealth. As Piketty notes, the low capital/income ratio "was in some ways a positive thing, in that it reflected in part a deliberate policy choice aimed to reduce ... the market value of assets and economic power of their owners."[8] Labor and social democratic policies—including higher taxes on dividends and profits, rent control policies, and new financial regulations just after World War II, played an important role in sustaining a new European regime far more egalitarian than the long prewar Belle Époque.

The same factors played out in this period in the United States, but the decline in the capital/income ratio was less dramatic. This partly reflects the lack of physical destruction on the homeland, but Piketty highlights other factors, including the high public debt expended to wage both world wars, which affected saving rates adversely. Most important, though, Piketty traces the history of public policy related to the New Deal, one of the few points where he expands on the crucial importance of state policy, especially the effect of taxes on income and wealth during this period. Because of the Depression, there was a willingness of Americans to dramatically increase taxes on both income and wealth, and move these taxes in a progressive direction, toward an almost confiscatory level on high income and wealthy people. "The top income tax rate rose to 63 percent in 1933 and then to 79 percent in 1937, surpassing the previous record of 1919. In 1942 the Victory Tax Act raised the top rate to 88 percent; and in 1944 it went up again to 94 percent. The top rate then stabilized at around 90 percent until the mid-1960s."[9] These astonishingly high tax rates on the rich obviously had the effect of significantly increasing equality, a preview of the policy that Piketty recommends today to reverse our current inequality.

War itself helped to enable these changes in taxes, since they were seen as necessary to win World War II, a much more popular war in the United States than subsequent American wars. FDR had to fight hard against the counterreaction by the rich, who called him "a traitor to his class," but they were not able to stop him.

War, though, was far from the only factor promoting the new tax policy—or the broader shift to greater equality. The other major factor was the Great Depression, which, of course, had links to European war and reparations policy toward Germany. The collapse of the US economy—and the rise of unemployment to higher than 25 percent—changed everything. The suffering of millions of workers led to a drastic change from the corporate regime of the 1920s to the New Deal in the 1930s. Beyond high taxes on the rich, the New Deal led to major new government stimuli, including direct government spending on job creation through the Works Progress Administration and the Civilian Conservation Corps. These job programs were part of the New Deal's partial but important successes in reducing inequality, and part of the era's economic exceptionalism.[10] Piketty mentions these government programs but gives them far too little attention—consistent with his general lack of an extended analysis of US state policies—despite their importance in reducing inequality.

World War II was a period of unprecedented government spending. Piketty discusses the effect of public debt and "victory taxes," but he doesn't say enough about the scale of public war spending. The American government spent more during World War II—at least $250 billion—than in all the prior years of the nation added together. This decisively pulled the country out of the Depression, reducing savings and creating major growth in the economy. This fueled equality and was consistent with the theory of military Keynesianism, or government spending to promote growth in the name of national security.[11]

After World War II, the persistence of very high military spending, and the continuation of New Deal policies, consolidated a long period of exceptional growth and rising equality that lasted until the 1970s. American victory in World War II was a huge factor in this American golden age, because the war essentially destroyed all major European and Japanese competition with the United States. The unprecedented military and economic dominance of the United States also meant that America set global financial rules favoring US economic interests, and the Cold War provided justification for US intervention that propped up governments friendly to American business. These were the spoils of war, and in that era, they promoted both American economic growth and rising equality.[12]

But much of the explanation for growth and equality in the post-war era was the institutionalization of New Deal policies. This involved high government spending to promote better social conditions at home: education for veterans, massive new interstate highways and other physical infrastructure, promotion of unions, and expansion of social welfare. These all contributed to a rise in wages and growth from the low point of the Depression.[13]

Nonetheless, many take from this period the lesson that it was largely war that pulled the nation out of Depression, and that war and military spending might be essential to promote equality and growth. Piketty does not make this argument, but others have.[14] In order that the lessons of the World War II era are not distorted, it is worth reflecting on the legacies of Vietnam and then the Reagan war regime, and the wars of Iraq and Afghanistan after 9/11. These are all eras of war that produced very different economic effects than World War II.[15] They expanded inequality rather than shrinking it, showing that it is not war per se that promotes equality or inequality but the political policies that may or may not be used during war eras. Very different policies are used in the name of war and prosperity, making the economic and social outcomes of war different in different eras. This is more consistent with the voice of Piketty 2, who emphasizes contingency and the role of politics and public policy. Because he does not spell out the argument related to American wars after World War II, which erase the conclusion that war is the best approach to growth and equality, we look briefly at these more recent wars.

The Vietnam War helped contribute to the end of high American growth and the golden era that built the middle class and more equality. Presidents Johnson and Nixon spent so much on the war that Nixon had to take America off the gold standard, as uncertainty about American debt and inflation destabilized financial conditions and led Wall Street to turn against the war. Vietnam diverted public funds into the military that might have been plowed into public investments in infrastructure, education, and economic development at home. As America was fighting in Vietnam, Germany and Japan were rebuilding their destroyed economies, prevented constitutionally from military spending and freed to invest in cars, electronics, and other manufacturing. Their growth rates soared in their "catch-up" phase as the US growth rate declined. All these conditions culminated after the war ended in 1975, in the US stagflation of the late 1970s that helped end the New Deal era.[16]

The election of Ronald Reagan in 1980 was a decisive turning point, revealing both the corrosive economic effects of war and war spending, especially when combined with the conservative policy agenda that Reagan locked into place and has now endured through the George W. Bush regime and beyond. The Reagan revolution perpetuated the military Keynesianism and ended the social Keynesianism that endured all through the post–World War II period, replacing a "guns and butter" policy with a "guns without butter" regime. It was intended to redistribute income and wealth to the rich, promoting a new reign of inequality similar to the Gilded Age, and it succeeded.[17]

The high military spending of the Reagan years, which continues through the present day, to be clear, has not re-created the same high growth rates spurred by World War II spending. They led to large military-driven deficits and were part of a foreign policy regime that continued to open up the world to American corporations that were increasingly committed to a global strategy of production, capitalizing on low wages, low taxes, and low regulation abroad. War spending diverted funding away from domestic public investment and social spending, part of a broader regime policy in which the wages and well-being of workers at home became a casualty of the pursuit of profits abroad, all leading to a new era of rising inequality and patrimonial capitalism.[18]

Central to this reconstruction of the Gilded Age was the Reagan revolution itself, an internal regime change in America that finished off the New Deal era and enshrined a new corporate regime. The new regime created the intertwined military and economic policies that led to a new extreme concentration of wealth and has become the foundation of the twenty-first-century patrimonial capitalism at the heart of Piketty's analysis. Remarkably, Piketty mentions Reagan and the Reagan revolution only three times in passing, a major omission. It reflects Piketty 1's immersion in the mechanistic economism detached from politics that he critiques so passionately at the outset of his work. Even a brief look shows that the economic effects of war and military spending are contingent not just on the scale of military spending or combat per se but on the broader economic and political agenda and policies in which wars are embedded.

Reagan's revolution aimed to redistribute wealth upward to the 1%, creating a new era of concentrated wealth and patrimonial capitalism. Reagan's first act in office was to destroy PATCO, the air-traffic-control union, a symbol of a concerted effort to destroy the labor movement that was the base of the New Deal. The attack on labor began with an attack on unions, but a vast arsenal of antilabor and antisocial welfare policies followed, combined with an extreme procorporate agenda. Reagan and his successors, especially George W. Bush, combined war with an attack on nearly all the pillars of the New Deal, including cutting public investment in jobs, infrastructure, education, and the environment.[19] At the same time, an attack on social welfare—including Social Security, Medicare, food stamps, education grants, affordable housing, public transportation, and public assistance—was carried out in the name of austerity and fiscal responsibility. Regulation of corporations and Wall Street was dismantled, adding to the reverse Robin Hood impact.

Meanwhile, the construction of a new 1% corporate class, capable of transmitting immense wealth to its children, was being cultivated through militarism making the world friendly to US business. US militarism was the iron fist facilitating the velvet glove of neoliberal or corporate trade and globalization policy facilitating corporate outsourcing of jobs, massive corporate welfare, systemwide deregulation of corporations and banking, elimination of campaign finance laws, and regressive tax policy drastically reoriented to favor the rich.[20]

The erosion of demand as wages fell and workers went into debt, along with deregulation of Wall Street and the housing industry, led to the 2008 Great Recession. The loss of wealth, which might have been theoretically equalizing, was countered by TARP and other massive bailouts to the rich, while workers losing their jobs, homes, or pensions were abandoned, with any funds that might have gone to rebuilding wages and the middle class wiped out by the $3 trillion investment in the wars in Iraq and Afghanistan.[21] It is strange that Piketty pays so little attention to all this, because it tells us so much about the political forces explaining the end of the midcentury unique "equality era" and connects the rise of a new militarized corporate system with extreme inequality and patrimonial capitalism.

Reagan's tax policy—and that of his successors—plays an especially important role that sheds light both on the economics of war and the creation of a reconstituted "inequality era" on steroids. One of Reagan's first acts was to reduce top income tax rates from close to 80 percent to 39 percent, followed by constant efforts by Reagan and his successors to reduce rates on the rich further, including efforts to eliminate corporate taxes altogether, reduce rates on income from capital, move toward a flat tax in the name of simplification, shift progressive income taxes to regressive sales taxes, and eliminate the estate tax, our main tax on wealth.[22]

Two factors stand out here. First, the equalizing effects of World War II were created partly by FDR's taxation of the rich, justified as "victory taxes" essential to the war effort. World War II made possible the very income and wealth taxes that hint at Piketty's current solutions. Yet Reagan's and Bush's wars led to exactly the opposite tax policies: drastically reducing taxes on the wealthy while burdening more the middle and working classes. This makes clear that war can lead toward equalizing policies and effects through taxation but can just as easily lead to extreme regressive tax policy and rising inequality. In either case, major economic effects are created not just by war and war spending but by the political agendas that surround them, in this case the contradictory impulses of the Franklin Roosevelt and Reagan regimes. Yet, it should also be clear that military Keynesianism (but not social Keynesianism) was key to both regimes, partly accounted for by the willingness of corporate elites in both eras to support high military spending.[23]

Second, the contradictory tax policies of the war regime of the mid-twentieth century versus those of the late twentieth century and early twenty-first century reinforce the idea that political policies surrounding war efforts are crucial in shaping the equalizing or unequalizing effects of war, as well as the health or sickness of the general economy. The New Deal, supported by military Keynesianism, produced the exceptional "equality era" that Piketty argues is entirely unique in the history of capitalism. The Reagan revolution, also embracing military Keynesianism, destroyed the midcentury "equality era" and led to economic collapse. The lesson is that World War II was unique, and hardly proof that militarism promotes equality and growth. To the contrary. The militarism reigning since Reagan seems to be more characteristic of the wars that we can expect in the future, ones linked to corporate-driven global military and trade policies that promote the forces of divergence over convergence and enshrine a new system of extreme inequality organized around a twenty-first-century militarized patrimonial capitalism.

What we need is an expanded conversation focusing on the relation between militarized and patrimonial capitalism. Piketty has set the table, but not really made this his issue. I have offered my own perspective on how and why the debate on this issue must be advanced. It's for academics, the peace movement, the labor movement, and the public to push this conversation to the next stage.

Discussion Questions

1. Does Piketty suggest that war, especially World War II, has been a key to American growth and prosperity?
2. Does his analysis suggest that war is necessary to promote growth and thus reduce inequality?
3. What are the main causes of American military interventions since World War II, and how do they relate to capitalism and the 1%?

4. Who profits from American wars? Does Piketty offer an answer? Is it the 1%? Is it the 99%?
5. What do the wars of Vietnam, Afghanistan, and Iraq tell us about the relation between war, economic growth, and inequality?
6. Is military Keynesianism an effective strategy to promote growth and equality?
7. Is there any economic or moral critique of US foreign policy in Piketty's analysis? Does he see the United States as imperialist?
8. Can Piketty's analysis be used to promote a critique of US militarism on either economic or moral grounds?

11

♦ ♦ ♦

THE CLIMATE OF CAPITALISM

What is the relation between US capitalism and climate change? Can you limit growth and consumption and still have more equality—and sustain capitalism? Or do we need to create a new economic model? Don't dominant capitalist classes require unfettered consumption—the fetishism of commodities—and haven't the working and poor classes become ardent fetishists? And how does the post-Piketty conversation reshape the politics and solution to climate change?

Piketty takes climate change very seriously, calling it "clearly the world's principal long-term worry."[1] His framework offers some new insights and questions about how the crisis can be approached. But his discussion of climate change is less than two pages. As with militarism and war, he cannot be expected to tackle every important issue in any depth. But given the seriousness of climate change, and the way in which his economic analysis could influence climate solutions, we need to see how his thinking might be factored into the climate conversation.

Despite his very short discussion, it is clear that Piketty sees, on economic grounds alone, great reason to worry about climate change. He believes the view of British climate policy expert Nicholas Stern that the economic damage will be so great in coming decades that it justifies spending at least 5 percent of GDP in coming years to mitigate the crisis.[2] Piketty says that public spending of this level would be unprecedented, and he argues it is unclear we would even know how to make such vast spending effective. Moreover, he calls the crisis more serious than even a carbon tax can solve, although he embraces a carbon tax, hinting that far deeper changes will be necessary to preserve our planet.[3]

Despite this important acknowledgment, he makes no serious effort to outline what such an agenda might look like, other than stressing that it will cost a lot of money and that we should not let concerns about the public debt deter us. He clearly believes that major government spending is necessary—and that solutions will require major technological and skills innovation. The most "urgent need," Piketty says, "is to increase our educational capital and prevent the degradation of our natural capital," without allowing the public debt to deter us in the rich nations, where we have such wealth. Public investment at high levels can be justified—and can promote equality—if it is accompanied by high taxes on the wealthy. He says, decisively: "The nations of Europe have never been so rich. What is true and shameful, on the other hand, is that this vast national wealth is very unequally distributed. Private wealth rests on public poverty."[4]

Piketty does not address the unique meaning of extreme inequality—and of patrimonial capitalism—in a climate-changed world. Of course, all classes and castes are ultimately vulnerable to climate change. But the 1% will be able to buy relief in the short- to mid-term, acquiring the highest and safest land and homes, above the floods below. They will have the money to do whatever it takes to get scarce resources and commodities. They can buy private security forces to protect from incursion by people displaced from low-lying land.

One might see in twenty-first-century patrimonial capitalism a form of climate caste. The very rich—the reigning 1% climate caste—will buy environmental, economic, and military security in a period of increasing climate-induced chaos. The disinherited majority caste—most of the 99%—will be locked into a life of increasing insecurity, scarcity, and violence. These are patterns that might occur without climate change, but they will be exacerbated intensely in a climate-changed world.

There are three other broad issues at the core of the climate discussion that Piketty doesn't discuss—and need urgent attention. Perhaps the most important is the question of growth. Growth is economists' religion, worshipped both among neoclassicists and Keynesians (and indeed many neo-Marxists). Growth is also central in Piketty's framework, since his whole analysis suggests that low-growth economics has historically been the recipe for high inequality. Because the return on capital tends to hover around 5 percent over centuries, low growth of 1 percent or less seems something that Piketty would view as problematic for any hope of moving toward a more equal and just society.

Even so, Piketty views low growth as the most likely reality of the twenty-first century. He projects a growth level of 1.2 percent in the wealthy countries, which he regards as "relatively optimistic," obviously concerned about inequality rather than climate change.[5] He does note that "this level of growth cannot be achieved, however, unless new sources of energy are developed to replace hydrocarbons, which are rapidly being depleted."[6] Yet it may be that his projection of relatively low growth, and his view that the real growth rates might be even lower, may explain why he doesn't discuss the need for even lower growth in the context of climate change. Perhaps he views realistic growth prospects sufficiently grim that one doesn't have to worry about growth as a continuing major contributor to the destruction of the environment.

Nonetheless, a growing number of political economists all over the world have taken a different position and argued that climate change cannot be stopped if we do not reduce growth substantially more, especially in the advanced countries.[7] This has led to arguments about "the limits of growth," with many climate economists and activists arguing that we need to move toward extremely limited or zero growth.[8] Rather than growth, we need to accept the novel idea of "sufficiency," which would lead us, at least in the advanced countries, to conclude that we already have more than enough material goods necessary for happiness.[9] Environmental economists have already shown our notions of growth and wealth are skewed toward market valuations that do not reflect personal happiness or real utility for people.[10] At minimum, this should lead to a conversation about what kind of growth promotes well-being, which would be growth in our public goods that are shrinking in our privatized commodity-led growth. Our growth is producing a wasteful accumulation of luxury and unnecessary goods and services while starving us of growth of essential public goods such as clean infrastructure, high-quality education, good child care, and good elder care.

Here, a Piketty 2 perspective could make a difference. It would promote a redefinition of the growth we need, one that dispenses with the wasteful growth satisfying the needs of the 1% and invests instead in the public goods that the 99% so desperately need. We need to show how the political power and cultural values of the 1% are promoting an unsustainable growth largely benefiting the 1% itself, growth in luxury goods and wasteful, status-oriented mass consumer goods at the expense of the rest of the population and the environment. One way to move toward equality is to invest heavily in public investment for public goods, a kind of growth that will simultaneously promote more equality, more environmental sustainability, and more public well-being. Piketty has laid the foundation for such a conversation, and his failure to discuss how growth needs to be redefined in the age of climate change—that increases equality and cleans up the environment—is one of the greatest limitations of his book.

To promote equality, beyond reducing commodity-led growth, we need to think globally. Any changes in growth would require reducing growth in the advanced countries while permitting it in the poorer nations, until an equitable balance in the standard of living around the world is achieved.[11] Moreover, a rapid move toward "ecological stimulus" and shift toward a global clean energy grid would permit such growth at least in the poor nations.[12] Reducing growth in rich nations and increasing it in poor countries could promote global equality while also helping mitigate climate change.[13]

But Piketty does not reassess, at least in *Capital in the Twenty-First Century*, his notion that growth is central to equality in the context of the climate change conversation. The only way that lower or zero growth would be consistent with promoting equality in rich nations would be a drastic population reduction or a historically unprecedented destruction of accumulated wealth, associated with an extremely rare reduction in the return on capital or created by a high wealth tax. The latter is Piketty's main solution to the problem of inequality, so it may be his view of how to reconcile growth and environmental protection. Presumably high wealth tax revenues could be used to generate massive public funds necessary to invest in an "eco-stimulus" and a rapid shift toward clean energy. But he also acknowledges that a high wealth tax is politically very difficult, leaving it unclear how to solve climate change in a high-growth environment.

When I interviewed Piketty, I asked him if the amount of growth necessary to reduce inequality is consistent with environmental sustainability. His response: "With the current technology, growth is not sustainable for very long. In theory it is possible to invent clean energy sources and have permanent immaterial growth, but we do not have these technologies yet. In any case, this won't solve $r > g$." What this seems to imply is that Piketty is in favor of rapid investment in clean energy technologies, to permit as much growth as possible consistent with sustainability. But he recognizes that those technologies have yet to be put in place on a scale commensurate with the problem. And it leaves open how he imagines that the rate of growth can be sustained to create more equality without destroying the environment.

We are left with the idea that reducing growth to deal with climate change may be tantamount to aiding and abetting extreme inequality, especially in a national context, such as in the United States. Low growth, in Piketty's framework, is a near guarantee of an unjust patrimonial capitalism. At minimum, if we embrace Piketty's framework, we need to hear how Piketty himself might see a solution to climate change in the context of future growth rates. Is he just counting on low growth rates or on politically unrealistic steep wealth taxes? Piketty does argue briefly in his book, and in interviews, that he supports a carbon tax, as well as major public investment to transit to a green economy. His view that it may be possible to move rapidly toward a clean energy infrastructure may underlie his lack of extended discussion about the climate change consequences of high growth. True, a totally green energy grid would permit at least modest rates of growth, consistent with slowing climate change. But the political prospects do not look hopeful, with the world, and especially the United States, being unwilling to sacrifice short-term profits flowing to Big Oil and Big Coal for the well-being of future generations.

The climate crisis might require, as neo-Marxists such as John Bellamy Foster have argued, moving entirely beyond our capitalist system,[14] a viewpoint that Piketty does not discuss or embrace, despite his readiness to discuss certain forms of democratic ownership of capital. Whether capitalism can survive in an era of zero growth—or one low enough to preserve the planet—is something that Piketty does not address but is crucially important. This is perhaps because he believes the better approach is to preserve growth while fighting for high wealth taxes and progressive investments in education and clean energy. In any case, he needs to make his views about growth in the context of climate change much clearer.

A closely related concern is limits on consumption. We live in mass consumer societies, and unfettered consumption is unquestionably a recipe for climate disaster.[15] We would need five to seven Earths to provide the resources if everyone in the world consumed at the per capita rate of individual consumption in the United States. A world of finite resources is incompatible with infinite consumption, and mass consumerism is undoubtedly a guarantee of climate disaster.[16]

Piketty makes no reference at all in his book to the need to limit consumption and does not bring it up in his discussion of climate change. He does very briefly discuss consumption taxes but dismisses them, among other reasons, as disproportionately burdensome on the poor—and thus unfair and unwelcome.[17] His emphasis on a global wealth tax, of course, as well as progressive income taxes, could limit the consumption of the very rich, but he does not explore the use of these taxes as a way specifically to reduce consumerism in the service of slowing climate change. Moreover, because consumption and growth are intertwined, any constraint on consumption would threaten growth, which would undermine Piketty's recipe for decreasing inequality.

Piketty's failure to even mention limiting consumerism in the context of the climate emergency is at odds with the sociological, cultural, and political sides of political economy that he argues for. Marxist sociologists—and other sociological and cultural analysts—have begun to call attention to what Marx called the "fetishism of commodities," the mystical attributes that capitalism ascribes to consumer products.[18] Much of the population has been imbued with this fetishism, and the mall is now the modern center of worship, a development clearly alarming in the context not only of climate change but the quality of public life.[19] Moreover, mass consumerism becomes increasingly untenable environmentally in the context of population growth, putting ever more unsustainable pressures on the environment.

At minimum, Piketty should have taken up shifts toward consumption of more sustainable public goods rather than carbon-intensive private goods. Bigger cars can be replaced by shared zip cars or public transportation. We don't have to imagine the end of consumption to save the planet but urgently need to consider essential and intelligent consumption that is sustainable and also consistent with human happiness.

Thorstein Veblen was the great classic theorist of consumption. His book *The Theory of the Leisure Class* is still as relevant and fresh today as when he wrote it more than a century ago. In the book, he introduces the famous idea of "conspicuous consumption," which points to the use of wasteful and exorbitant consumption as a major way for people in modern capitalism to display their status.[20]

Veblen observes that consuming has become a primary way that people in modern capitalism establish their worth. This is exploited most by the rich, who have the discretionary income and wealth to buy the exorbitant commodities that command attention and respect, whether a palatial estate or a $30,000 watch. While conspicuous consumption infects the working class as well, it metastasizes into what he calls "invidious consumption" among the wealthy, where unfettered consumerism pollutes the entire social (and natural) landscape and moves the society into a sickness of narcissistic wastefulness, all in the service of displaying one's superior status.

The connections with Piketty and his concept of the wealthy in patrimonial capitalism are rich with possibilities, and it is a shame that Piketty mentions Veblen only once, in a footnote.[21] The conspicuous and invidious consumption of the leisure class is, first, a window into the caste realities of modern capitalism. The "new money" capitalists of his age, as Veblen points out, were obsessed with the need to display their "essence," or superior being, by taking on the manners of the old European nobility. The Gilded Age robber barons—the Rockefellers, Vanderbilts, Carnegies, and others—thus spent extravagantly on their Newport summer "cottages" that aped the castles of the European aristocracy. They also dressed in exaggerated finery and ate at great tables loaded with excess and served by butlers in tuxedos in their Fifth Avenue New York palatial residences. Matthew Josephson, the great social observer of the robber barons, in his wonderful work *The Robber Barons* confirms this view of the Gilded Age capitalists as obsessed with claiming not just the wealth but the caste status of the Old Europe nobility.[22]

Veblen and Josephson are offering a vivid view—the social science equivalent of the portraits by Balzac and Austen in Belle Époque Europe—of the social and cultural realities of patrimonial capitalism. The wealthy are a caste, which, lacking the divine claims of the Middle Ages about superior being, relies on conspicuous and invidious consumerism to establish its superior essence. Conspicuous consumption is essentially a "caste class" strategy of the 1% to affirm its claims of divine worth, one in the climate change era that spells disaster.

There is a trickle-down effect on the disinherited 99%. They want to use whatever discretionary income they have to rank themselves relative to others within their caste class. So conspicuous consumption becomes the form of invidious competition for what the French theorist Pierre Bourdieu calls "cultural capital," the mark of special worth or breeding. Competing for cultural capital through consumerism is now a leading competitive drive for the 99%, emulating the 1% to enhance their own status. It leads to a sociopathic struggle of each against all to affirm relative worth and power, and divide the 99% against each other.[23]

Beyond the intriguing insights into caste behavior, the arguments by Veblen and Bordieu have major implications for climate change. Where competition for status and power is driven by conspicuous consumption, the crisis of climate change is clearly exacerbated. Any restraints on consumption become a threat to identity and one's sense of worth.

It is hard to imagine a solution to climate change in a world where identity and self-esteem are measured by conspicuous consumption. Veblen treated conspicuous consumption as a form of sociopathy in the pursuit of status, without recognizing the sociopathic threat it represents toward nature and future generations. This is where Piketty 2 might have stepped in, particularly since he tells us that Bordieu was one of the French intellectuals that he most admired and wanted to study with.[24]

The problem of climate change is forever entangled with the culture of caste and conspicuous consumption. There will only be mitigation of climate change when a cultural shift occurs that reduces the status and caste anxieties of both the wealthy and the workers, driving them both to unsustainable consumerism, especially the rich. Any such culture change will be formidably different in the era of patrimonial capitalism, showing how deeply the Piketty analysis needs to be probed and adapted to explore solutions to the climate crisis.

A third problem regarding Piketty and climate change is the lack of any extended discussion of market externalities. All market transactions have externalized costs and benefits—and environmental economics has long made them a central focus. Yet Piketty, while obviously entirely familiar with the problem of externalities, offers little insight about how to deal with them, especially such catastrophic externalities as those leading to climate change, although his discussion of carbon taxes is an implicit recognition of the need to "internalize" the externalized cost of destroying our "natural capital."

Inequality itself can be seen as a form of market externality. Because Piketty highlights that extreme inequality can flow from "perfectly operating" markets, it is strange that he doesn't highlight the problem of externalities as a part of his analysis of inequality, one of the greatest of social externalities. Just as he shows that power of corporate executives helps shape the labor market, it is important that political power by the 1% broadly helps determine what kinds of externalities are recognized and corrected through taxation or other measures. It is obvious in the United States that the failure to address climate change—the most deadly of all market externalities—reflects political influence by large oil and coal companies as well as by much of the corporate community and their supporters in Congress.[25]

Dealing with climate change requires a focus, then, on precisely the political factors that Piketty argues are critical for political economists to discuss. That would require a broader political critique of how the 1% helps construct the market, and an extended reflection on how markets can deal with both social and environmental externalities. Piketty is largely silent on this issue, beyond his focus on taxes (certainly a major way to deal with externalities and possibly consumerism), and he does not offer any new insights about how political forces create environmental externalities or how to solve them. This is where the twenty-first-century conversation must go well beyond Piketty—in a broader critique of market economics than Piketty offers, though one hopes that he will contribute here.

A "new economics" is developing in the United States and else-where, recognizing the urgency of discussing and solving the problem of externalities while also undermining the mass religion of consumerism.[26] It is important to see whether Piketty's framework can be adapted to add to this crucial new model of thinking. Creating more equality—for example, through high wealth taxes or higher wages—without address-ing consumerism could easily increase mass consumption, thus adding to the gravity of the climate change crisis, with even greater intensity as population grows.

Climate change must be a vital part of the new conversation about inequality and patrimonial capitalism that Piketty has begun. We ur-gently need to replace private goods or consumer products with public goods.[27] The rise in private wealth and a caste-based society may be an important way to help shift the conversation about our cultural values and our stress on consumerism as the way to the good life. Piketty himself seems sympathetic to a renewed focus on public goods, and thus could play an important role in this new conversation. Let's hope he chimes in.

Discussion Questions

1. Is climate change linked to inequality? If so, how?
2. Can we have economic growth and still stop climate change?
3. Would limiting economic growth and consumption inevitably create more inequality?
4. Is there a way, within Piketty's framework, to accept zero growth and still move toward more equality?
5. Could revenues from a wealth tax be used to massively increase public investment in clean energy?
6. Is Piketty a potential important voice in the movement to stop climate change? If so, why?
7. Is Piketty, despite his embrace of a carbon tax, too locked into traditional ideas of growth to help move us urgently to climate change solutions?

♦ ♦ ♦

READING CAPITAL IN
THE ANTHROPOCENE

JULIET B. SCHOR

apital in the Twenty-First Century is a magnificent book. Thomas Piketty has taken on central questions about capitalism and succeeded brilliantly, offering a long overdue resuscitation of political economy. Classical nineteenth-century political economists put distribution at the center of their analyses of growth, unlike the later neoclassicals who pushed distribution to the side. At a time when inequalities of income and wealth are returning to historic pre–World War II levels, it is vital to understand what is happening and why. The painstaking efforts of Piketty and his collaborators have yielded pioneering data sets that form the basis of a novel interpretation of the capital accumulation process over two and a half centuries.

Piketty is also to be commended for his courage. He has harsh words for the economics profession, calling it childish, absurd, detached from other social sciences, and wrongly thinking of itself as engaged in "science." These are warranted criticisms, but economists are a clannish group. Few within the fraternity are as outspoken as he has been. But his willingness to go against the grain, and to combine sophisticated economic theory with old-fashioned history, slogs through the data, and practical thinking has resulted in such an important contribution.

Personally, I have found my ideas about growth and distribution permanently changed by Piketty's work. And these are topics that I spent quite a bit of time on earlier in my career, particularly as part of an international group of economists who were looking at many of the topics that Piketty takes up, such as trends in the capital/labor ratio, productivity, and how distribution affects growth.[1] Some will be tempted to find out what all the fuss is about by confining themselves to the extensive reviews and commentary on the book—those who resist will be well rewarded by a text that is both engaging and enlightening.

One dimension of the book I found curious, however, is its lack of attention to the implications of living in a unique geologic era: the Anthropocene. (For those unfamiliar with the term, it refers to the current epoch, in which for the first time in history, humans are profoundly altering the earth's climate, and by extension its basic ecosystems.) Surely the fact that the global economy is on a trajectory to add four degrees of warming (Centigrade) before century's end, with a high probability of attendant catastrophes, is relevant for thinking about capital accumulation.

There's a growing literature that reinterprets the history of the industrial age through the lens of fossil fuels and material flows. This new paradigm relies on material flows rather than flows of value to understand how industrial capitalism has grown and developed. I refer here to the work of scholars such as Robert Ayres, Marina Fischer-Kowalski, and Helmut Haberl and historians such as E. A. Wrigley, who pioneered the well-known distinction between organic and mineral economies. Not surprisingly, fossil fuel energy plays a central role in these accounts, given that it is the key input that yields the phenomenal productivity increases of the modern era. As I read *Capital in the Twenty-First Century*, I wondered about the role of energy, and other resources, such as biomass.

There's an important connection between the work of these historians and Piketty's narrative, as well as to the rapidly expanding literatures on ecological overshoot, climate destabilization, and limits to growth. A central conclusion of the book is that the rate of return on capital typically exceeds the rate of growth of the economy ($r > g$) and that under these conditions wealth accumulates at the top of the distribution. The greater the divergence between the two rates, the more unequal the distribution becomes. The message of many scientists is that we have already reached the limits of growth for a large number of key ecosystems and resources. Global warming is the most well known, but excessive aerosol loading, ocean acidification, species biodiversity, water use, human appropriation of net primary productivity, and toxic emissions also result from economic growth.

In wealthy countries a conversation has begun about the need to reduce economic growth. It is most developed in Europe, where growth is no longer taken for granted. In Piketty's home country of France, advocates of *décroissance,* or de-growth, are very much on the Left, and not well integrated into the policy conversation, but in other countries the conversation is taking place within mainstream circles. It is probably worth noting that the de-growth position does not advocate this path for countries of the global South; a fundamental principle is that wealthy countries have already used their fair shares of global ecological resources and they should now begin to radically reduce their ecological and carbon footprints. De-growthers are aligned with climate scientists who, like Piketty, are putting hard numbers on concepts that others prefer to leave fuzzy. Rich countries must achieve "radical emissions reductions" of approximately 10 percent per annum over the next few decades if we are to have any chance of averting catastrophic climate change via a path that pays attention to global equity. So far, we haven't figured out a way to do this while still expanding the size of the economy, a point that has been made by many.

The vital lesson from Piketty's book, which has mostly not been recognized by the anti-growth camp, is that slower GDP expansion will lead to concentration of wealth at the top through the $r > g$ mechanism. De-growthers are well aware of a variety of other bad consequences that can result from unmanaged slowdowns, such as rising unemployment and poverty. But they have not yet come to terms with this additional, fearsome consequence of the steady state.

Growing inequality is not only a problem for its social, economic, and human impacts. There is also a small but expanding literature suggesting that inequality itself drives ecological degradation. The work of economist James Boyce is noteworthy here. Boyce finds that in the United States, states that have more unequal distributions of income and political power are more likely to have worse environmental outcomes and a weaker policy regime. Perhaps the most obvious example of how inequality can create tragic environmental outcomes is the outsized political influence of the fossil fuel industry on US policy, at both the state and federal levels.

Conversely, there are important questions to be asked about how capital accumulation will proceed in the Anthropocene. Piketty's story is mainly one of continuity, from the late eighteenth century to the present. To be sure, there are national differences, and politics and institutions matter in his account, but he identifies strong tendencies across times and places. The prominent exception to the continuity narrative is the impact of the Great Depression and World War II. These events led to the collapse of the capital stock and an anomalous period. (Understanding the post-WWII period as aberrant, rather than normative, is now more broadly recognized in the social sciences.) The question about the future, then, is whether ecological pressures will create the equivalents of the twentieth-century traumas.

There is accumulating evidence that climate disruption will have serious negative consequences for water supplies, agricultural yields, sea level rise, fish populations, vector-borne diseases, and extreme weather events. The productivity of land is projected to decline in many parts of the world, which in turn will affect its price. Ocean productivity is collapsing and with it the major protein source for roughly a billion people. If climate change leads to large numbers of refugees and declines in food production, the economic disruption that occurs is likely to create sharp reductions in the market value of capital. Similarly, extreme weather events destroy capital. A further effect is that built capital or machinery that relies on an outmoded energy source is devalued with a shift to a new energy technology.

And finally, there's the impact of the so-called carbon bubble. This refers to the idea that fossil fuel companies have trillions of assets on their books that are unusable if the planet is to stay within its carbon budget and avoid catastrophic climate impacts. A recent estimate suggests that 60–80 percent of priced fossil fuel reserves are unburnable, and that current equity valuations could be reduced by 40–60 percent as a result. Given that these companies currently represent $4 trillion in valuation, and at current rates of growth will make $6 trillion more in investments over the next decade,[2] it seems likely that there will be a major write-down in these companies' valuations. If there isn't, we'll have far bigger problems, namely survival on an inferno planet.

Is climate change taking us into another period of dramatic capital destruction? And if it is, how do we want to respond? Is another "golden age" of compressed inequality and an expanding welfare state possible? Perhaps out of disaster we can build the public wealth that Piketty shows has become so negligible but that is essential in a world where common ecological resources are so critical. In the post-WWII period, the West was able to mount a relatively democratic, egalitarian response to the widespread destruction of capital. Can we manage this today, and if so, can we also make it ecologically sustainable?

At the beginning of the book Piketty writes that economists need to engage with other social scientists. As we look forward to the coming decades of the Anthropocene, it seems obvious that there is a related imperative to engage with natural scientists—ecologists, climate scientists, and biologists, among others. *Capital in the Twenty-First Century* is an inspiring example of the extraordinary fruits that such collaborations can produce.

12

◆ ◆ ◆

CAPITALISM VS. DEMOCRACY

Are capitalism and democracy compatible? Can democracy coexist with great concentrations of wealth? Does the capitalist governing class rule America? How might the post-Piketty world change the political conversation about money and politics—and about democracy itself? Does it offer promise of a new or stronger set of movements for limiting corporate power and empowering citizens and movements for democracy?

On page 1 of his book, Piketty writes that "as it did in the nineteenth century and seems quite likely to do again in the twenty-first, capitalism automatically generates arbitrary and unsustainable inequalities that radically undermine the meritocratic values on which democratic societies are based."[1] This undermines the most important consensus in Western societies: that capitalism and democracy go hand in hand, and that the former is necessary to achieve the latter. If we do not have freedom in the market, presumably what capitalist societies offer, we cannot have freedom in our society.[2]

Piketty is very clear about his commitments to democracy, which motivate his study of inequality and capitalism. He says in his book, "If we are to regain control of capitalism, we must bet everything on democracy."[3] The central—and most provocative—thesis of his work is that the structure of capitalism offers no guarantees that it will support democracy. In fact, he leans toward the idea that without extraordinary political interventions, the "perfect operation" of the markets will lead to inequality outcomes inconsistent with the preservation of a true democracy.[4]

Piketty—and this is the voice of Piketty 2—asserts definitively that "real democracy and social justice require specific institutions of their own, not just those of the market, and not just parliaments and other formal democratic institutions."[5] This is a strong statement, and it hints at the need for deep structural change in the market system and our current "democratic" politics to achieve true democracy. While it is a crucially important theme in the book, it has not been picked up widely, perhaps because Piketty does not develop the point at great length and one has to tease it out of many different parts of his argument.

Piketty hints at several serious and potentially antidemocratic aspects of markets. But the most important is the historical tendency for the forces of divergence to triumph over those of convergence, creating lasting and excessive inequality. While the triumph of r over g is not an iron law, it is Piketty's overriding concern, and he worries most that it bodes poorly for democracy. As the return on capital exceeds the rate of growth, as it has over many centuries, wealth will grow faster than wages and the wealthy, over time, will become rentiers, whose increasing inherited fortunes grow at an accelerating rate with their size.[6] The largest fortunes grow faster than smaller ones, and faster than the wages and savings of workers. On average, in the long run, inherited wealth will "dominate wealth amassed from a lifetime's labour by a wide margin." It is no surprise that Piketty takes this swipe at a rising caste society: "the Rentier, Enemy of Democracy."[7]

Piketty clearly fears that extreme inequality—both of income and wealth—can subvert democracy. Money is power. If wealth concentrates in fewer and fewer hands, the income and wealth gaps between the top classes and all others grow very large. With the growth in economic inequality comes, inevitably, a growth in power inequality, potentially dooming democracy. This is hardly a new or controversial idea. As Justice Louis Brandeis famously said, "You can have great wealth and you can have democracy, but you can't have both."[8]

By showing that capitalism has strong inherent tendencies toward extreme inequality and dynastic fortunes, Piketty has redefined the debate about the future of democracy. It is not simply that extreme inequality concentrates huge pots of money in the 1% that pollute politics and ensure plutocracy. The argument is interesting because it is more original, tied to his central argument about the rise of inherited wealth in patrimonial democracy. His basic thesis is the fundamental incompatibility between a caste society and democracy.

His argument thus goes beyond the general and familiar argument about tensions between inequality and democracy. It points to the specific antidemocratic tendencies of patrimonial capitalism—with its strong antimeritocratic, caste character.[9] This is where the conversation after Piketty has to go.

The incompatibility of a caste society and democracy needs to be explained clearly. Caste societies presume fundamental differences in the "essences" or blood of various parts of the population. Those with superior essences are entitled to different and more expansive rights than those who are inferior. This has obvious political implications.

Superior beings are vested in caste society—whether in feudal society, the Indian caste system, or the antebellum slave American South—with rights to govern. Caste inequality is such a deep human distinction or division that it cannot be reconciled with equal rights or democracy, because the common interest is served by empowering those equipped by blood or God to rule. Caste societies have historically been autocratic, depriving lower castes of any right to govern but typically presuming a "noblesse oblige," in which the upper castes will protect the inferior and rule in the interests of both themselves and lower castes.

In caste capitalism, the political calculation becomes more complex, because capitalism ideologically rejects birth or caste as an organizing political principle. Capitalism claimed to liberate people from chains of caste and open opportunity to all, who deserved the rights to prove their merit through hard work and success on the market. Its legitimacy rested on its repudiation of the ancient privileges of birth and blood.

This is where Piketty's approach offers a new wedge for advocates of democracy. A caste-based capitalism violates capitalism's own ideological or moral principles. When caste is merged with class, as in patrimonial capitalism, the crisis of democracy is heightened as the melding of caste and class inequalities increases barriers to democracy. This is one of the reasons that Piketty champions democracy so strongly and argues that it requires forceful political intervention to move markets and capitalism itself into democratic alignment.

Piketty thus brings his wealth tax and other interventions to reduce caste class inequality as, most important, a means of creating true democracy. He is not making an argument against modest inequality (which may be consistent with democracy) but only for a level consistent with promoting general utility or the common good,[10] a philosophical position he takes based on the 1789 Declaration of the Rights of Man, and discussed more in the next chapter. Because democracy is clearly a common good, and capitalism historically leans toward extreme inequality, the debate about democracy suddenly becomes tied to a debate about capitalism. Neoclassical economists, such as Milton Friedman, have tried to end this argument for good, by reasoning that free markets are the absolute foundation of democracy, and virtually guarantee it, a view Piketty completely rejects.[11]

Marx made the argument about democracy in capitalism quite differently in the nineteenth century, asserting that democracy was a fig leaf invented by capitalists to legitimate the capitalist system. Marx contended, famously, that government in capitalism is nothing but "the executive committee of the bourgeoisie."[12] It could not be otherwise, because control of production and wealth ensures political power. Marx believed that capitalists had, in his own lifetime, gained control over the material foundation of society—the means of production—and that they had used that power to control not just business but the state, the "superstructure" that provided the necessary laws, military force, and ideological control that sustained capitalism itself.[13] For the Scientific Marxist this was an iron law. For the Critical Marxist it was contingent; workers could gain significant influence in the state because it has "relative autonomy." But even Critical Marxists have believed that workers could never control the state within capitalism itself.[14]

Piketty is not either type of Marxist. As a Keynesian economist, he argues that capitalism and democracy can coexist, never suggesting that capitalism should be replaced with another system to achieve substantive democracy, despite the obstacles posed by patrimonial capitalism.[15] He says at the outset, "There are nevertheless ways democracy can regain control over capitalism and ensure that the general interest takes precedence over private interests."[16] But his analysis of the tendencies operating in a capitalist "perfect market," which has no forces that naturally limit concentration of wealth, means that there will always be serious tension between capitalism and democracy. And these tensions are rooted, at least for Piketty 2, not just in inequality but in broader concerns about the structure and operations of markets and society in patrimonial capitalism. It will take significant political intervention to resolve those tensions and ensure that patrimonial capitalism does not doom democracy.

For the majority of economists who embrace the happy Kuznets thesis that capitalism over the long run distributes the fruits of production across most of the society, Piketty is promoting an unnecessary conversation, smacking more than a bit of heresy. If capitalism has inherent tendencies to spread wealth and promote only modest and justifiable inequality, with caste destroyed by mobility and opportunities built into the markets, then capitalism and democracy are soul mates and coexist without any serous tension. But by rejecting the Kuznets thesis, Piketty has started a potentially dangerous new conversation.

How heretical or dangerous that conversation might be depends on two factors. One is about the variety of forces in capitalism itself—including inequality and caste integral to patrimonial capitalism—that may subvert democracy. The second is how much political intervention is required to ward off extreme inequality and a deepening caste order, and what is required to change other antidemocratic market forces to make capitalism "the slave of democracy rather than the reverse."

First, extreme inequality leading toward a caste society is the most important antidemocratic force. The problem here is that the greater the inequality, the more likely the rise of significant inherited wealth in a society of rentiers.[17] Elites in such a society may claim meritocratic values but will use those values as an ideology to disguise their ability to control the state with their vast fortunes. Patrimonial capitalism will still operate with voting and "procedural democracy," but substantive democracy will be eroded if not destroyed by the sheer volume of inherited wealth commanded by the few, and the creation of a disinherited caste majority made up of the mass of people who may vote—using "procedures" of democracy—but can never get their voices truly heard.

The role of caste in patrimonial societies is incompatible with democracy. Caste divisions in the Middle Ages created permanent and legalized divisions between the powerful and the powerless. Caste classes in patrimonial capitalism remove the legal obstacles to universal voting but put in place a more invisible block to democracy. It appears that everyone is on an equal playing field, but the overwhelming weight of inherited wealth and caste help the past "consume the present," in Piketty's words, thus giving accumulated fortunes the ability to overcome in the real political world any legal claim to equal rights.[18]

The democratic crisis of patrimonial capitalism is closely related to a set of other, related antidemocratic elements in the markets, which are especially evident in Piketty 2's voice. Neoclassical economists have largely embraced the idea that the markets are inherently a form of democratic institution because they involve voluntary exchange, in contrast to the coercive dictate of the state. In a free market, within the neoclassical framework, fundamental rights of private property and free choice are ensured.[19] Nobody tells you what product to buy on the shelf or who you have to work for. You make your own decisions about what to buy or sell. Nobody can infringe on the liberty guaranteed by the institutions of private property and the market itself. Moreover, competition ensures that economic power does not concentrate; competition ensures, if not perfect equality of power, an almost invincible buffer against any actor or group of actors taking charge in the market itself. And it is this institutional essence of the market that guarantees democracy and liberty, because the market itself protects the opportunity of every citizen to make his or her own choices, enshrining as fundamental social values the individual freedom at the heart of democracy. Moreover, economic competition in the market nurtures and helps ensure the decentralized power also essential to political democracy. In short, markets embody, inspire, and protect political freedoms, including the choice of one's own speech and political candidates.[20]

While Piketty 1 embraces much of this thinking, Piketty 2 implicitly questions it. Piketty 2 argues that the market—especially the labor market that he focuses on in some detail—is "a social construction," and that the rules of the market are not inherently democratic but reflect the power of governing groups.[21] For Piketty 2, markets are as varied as the societies in which they are embedded, and freedom is not inherent in the market, nor can capitalism ensure that whatever market freedoms exist will translate into political freedoms and democracy. In other words, contrary to the economic consensus, markets have no inherent values or structural rules that diffuse power or ensure freedom, either in the market itself or in politics.

This Piketty 2 perspective—about the role of power in "free markets"—is especially evident in his analysis of the wage market of top executives. Recall that Piketty rejects the theory of marginal productivity in his discussion of the pay of "super-managers." Instead, he argues that top executives have the power to set their own salaries, replacing the invisible hand with their own quite visible "hands in the till."[22]

Piketty 2 raises questions about the theory of marginal productivity in other groups, emphasizing that it is always difficult to judge productivity and that social mores and "bargaining power" always play a role.

While the marginal productivity of relatively unskilled workers—burger flippers or janitors—may make their productivity easier to judge, Piketty argues that social values and bargaining power always come into play[23] and affect perceptions about productivity, as is obvious in recent strikes by minimum-wage workers around the United States. And, as noted earlier in our discussion of nursing home aides, the very perception of skill is socially constructed, with the color and gender of caretakers a large factor in shaping the view of their productivity. The same could be said of child-care workers or social workers. All of this tells us that markets are not operating simply by abstract laws of marginal productivity but by social rules and power.

Once the market is accepted as a social construction, any notion of it as an inherently democratic institution evaporates. First, there is no "inherent feature," because markets vary in all societies. Second, the judgments or valuations of the market are so permeated by ruling social values and power that there is little free about them; they reflect power dynamics that are bred in the market itself, and in the larger society that radiate back into the market. Moreover, the growing ability of very large companies—that are oligopolies or monopolies to dictate their own terms—suggests that the concentration of power within the markets is very high and growing. Moreover, as the political power of large corporations grows very large, through input of billions of dollars into electoral campaigns and lobbying, it becomes obvious that US markets are operating in ways that undermine rather than support democracy.[24]

This takes us back to the inequality issue. If markets tend to produce extreme inequality, it will clearly reinforce all these other antidemocratic aspects of capitalism. And both Piketty 1 and 2 see the markets as having no inherent features limiting inequality. Both Pikettys also see strong forces over the long term promoting very high inequality and a dominant sway of inherited wealth, suggesting that the social constructions we call the market will be ever more shaped by tip-top caste classes operating both within the market and via state power that they control.

This leads to the second question about the intensity of Piketty's heresy: How much political intervention is required to ward off extreme inequality and related antidemocratic market forces? And how realistic or utopian are the prospects of success?

Keynesian economists have long recognized that political intervention is necessary to stabilize and preserve capitalism. But, as discussed by leading Keynesians such as Paul Krugman, these have been seen as "magneto" or coordination problems that are not of great complexity.[25] Krugman compares the problems of the economy to the routine problems of an aging car; you find a good mechanic and he will fix the problem with a good degree of reliability. With the right Keynesian interventions, the problems of extreme inequality, dynastic wealth in patrimonial capitalism, and other antidemocratic issues should be equally easy to fix.[26]

Krugman, of course, recognizes that simple policy solutions are not politically easy, a view shared by many Keynesians. Yet the presumption is that, over the long run, the political will can be mobilized, partly because of the assumption that we live in a capitalist democracy, even if a flawed one, in which people can eventually exercise enough influence over government, as in the New Deal, to hire an excellent team of Keynesian mechanics. Keynesian reforms will obviate the need for a revolution and prevent economic collapse; Keynesians will be able to help save capitalism from itself.

Piketty 1 seems aligned with Krugman. The problems are solvable within capitalism. The forces of divergence are strong, but there are clear solutions, and history suggests that the political will to implement them, as exemplified in the New Deal and European social democracy, can and will be mobilized.

Piketty 2 is less certain. He notes that history does not suggest optimism about the triumph of convergence over divergence. His prognosis about the rise of extreme concentrations of inherited wealth in the twenty-first century does not suggest politically infectious hope. He makes political proposals—and is personally involved in trying to implement them. But he notes the political complexities and views the political contingencies as highly uncertain. He realizes the 1% will resist large-scale solutions involving redistribution and taxes, or limiting the role of money in politics. Moreover, his political solutions may not rise to the scale of the democratic problems we face, an issue we turn to in the final two questions.

The failure to develop a serious historical and political analysis of how corporate forces in the United States and worldwide have undermined democracy is a shortcoming of Piketty's work. There is, of course, already a great deal of work in the United States on corporate power and its threats to democracy, going back to a very strong tradition of critical political sociology led by C. Wright Mills and G. William Domhoff.[27] But the corporate or 1% subversion of democracy is so central to Piketty's main concern with inequality and patrimonial capitalism that it needs to be addressed, and it would be very important for him, in later work, to take up these issues within the context of his own analysis.

The omission is serious, first, because of his overwhelming commitment to democracy, and, second, because of the force of his explicit argument that extreme inequality and the caste character of patrimonial capitalism are serious threats to sustaining a democratic society. As I have emphasized repeatedly, and show in more depth in the last two chapters, Piketty does not follow through on the importance that he attaches to political analysis in his initial discussions. In regard to democracy, there is virtually no discussion of how corporations poison the democratic well, whether through massive infusion of money into elections, intense lobbying, threats of capital flight or exit, influence of executive and judicial decisions favoring corporate over labor interests, and taxation policy itself. Nor is there the extended discussion that is necessary about the historical role caste societies play in destroying democracy and the new ways that this will likely be manifested in the patrimonial capitalism of the twenty-first century.

Nonetheless, when I asked him about the democratic crisis, and the compatibility between great wealth and democracy, Piketty gave a memorable response that would suggest he recognizes the great problems and also sees political possibilities to make a difference if we choose to do so: "Capitalism can be the slave of democracy, or the opposite, but one has to choose."

Discussion Questions

1. Can patrimonial capitalism be democratic?
2. Put another way, can a society marked by dynastic wealth and extreme inequality be a true democracy?
3. Are there very serious tensions in Piketty's analysis of inequality between capitalism and democracy?
4. Is government always going to be controlled by the 1%?
5. Does the power of super-managers to set their own salaries in the United States doom both equality and democracy?
6. Does a caste class system doom democracy?

7. What do you think Piketty means when he says, "Capitalism can be the slave of democracy, or the opposite, but one has to choose." Does that imply optimism about democratic prospects?

13

♦ ♦ ♦

THE SOCIAL STATE AND
ECONOMIC DEMOCRACY

Does Piketty redefine the politics we need, and does his analysis suggest a challenge to patrimonial capitalism, or to capitalism itself? Piketty is most widely known for his proposal for a global wealth tax, but he hints at a broader proposal to democratize the ownership of capital. Since Piketty is not a Marxist, what does he have in mind when he calls for—and spells out briefly—a variety of ways to spread wealth and democratize capital? How do his endorsements of the UN Declaration of Rights and the European "social state" fit into his call for tax reform, for spreading wealth and democratizing capital? Is he arguing that economic democracy is necessary for political democracy?

When it comes to solutions, people focus largely on Piketty's proposal for a global wealth tax. Taxes do play a big role in Piketty's policy prescriptions. He argues that more progressive income taxes as well as new wealth taxes can have a major impact on reducing inequality, warding off new global economic crises, and building democracy.[1]

But while Piketty himself has put forward the global wealth tax as a centerpiece of his political agenda, he sets the table by talking more broadly about the need for expanding "democratic control of capital." This has a Marxist ring, but we have already seen that Piketty is not a Marxist and is not seeking to replace capitalism with communism, socialism, or government control of the means of production. This leads to the question of what Piketty has in mind when he discusses democratic control of capital—and what, beyond the wealth tax, would lead in that direction? Most commentators on Piketty have largely ignored that question, but it is key to the politics that Piketty's work opens up.

Piketty starts the political conversation by saying that he believes in the "social state" rather than socialism. By the social state, he is referring to the democratic advanced states, especially in Europe, that have embraced a philosophy of human rights and a mix of public and private ownership, including a far more expansive role for the state than existed in earlier centuries. The social state is not based on government ownership of production, but it does involve a large role for government and growing commitment to innovative forms of democratic control of capital—and spreading wealth—in ways to be discussed shortly.[2]

The "social state" is based on the French Revolution's 1789 Declaration of the Rights of Man and the Citizen. Piketty returns repeatedly to this Declaration, which proclaims that "men are born free and remain free and equal in rights."[3] Piketty's politics are grounded in this notion of equality of rights, which the social state is organized to protect.[4]

But what does such "equality of rights" truly entail, and how is it related to democratic ownership of capital? Piketty argues that the Declaration shifts the "burden of proof" to those proposing any inequality: "equality is the norm, and inequality is acceptable only if based on 'common utility.'"[5] This means that "social inequalities are acceptable only if they are in the interest of all and in particular of the most disadvantaged social groups."[6] Piketty continues, "Hence basic rights and material advantages must be extended in so far as possible to everyone, as long as it is in the interest of those who have the fewest rights and opportunities to do so."[7]

Piketty argues this is consistent with the social ethics and political philosophy of the moral philosopher John Rawls as well as the Indian economist Amartya Sen, both known for egalitarian sympathies.[8] But notice, as well, the similarity to Karl Marx, also a child of the Enlightenment who championed equal rights prioritizing the disadvantaged. One sees this Marx-like sensibility further in Piketty's commentary on the failure of nineteenth-century US and European societies to live up to their philosophy of equal rights: "The US and French Revolutions both affirmed equality of rights as an absolute principle—a progressive stance at the time. But in practice, during the nineteenth century, the political systems that grew out of those revolutions concentrated mainly on the protection of property rights."[9] This is surely a critique that Marx would heartily endorse.

Piketty argues that the meaning of "equal rights" is ultimately a democratically contested question—now central in twenty-first-century patrimonial capitalism—about the scope of universal rights required to protect especially the "most disadvantaged." The "common utility" standard says no inequality should be tolerated unless serving the interest of all. Piketty acknowledges this may mean political intervention to provide a very broad set of social and economic rights, beyond the rights to education, health, and pensions now embraced by the European social state. He says that the twenty-first century might decide to include equal rights "to culture, housing, and travel" as a complement to the twentieth-century embrace of equal rights to health care, education, and pensions.[10]

Piketty opens here a potentially expansive view of the social state, requiring a considerable spread of wealth and democratic control of capital. But what rights in the twenty-first century will be embraced for all is, he says, a subject of intense democratic conflicts. "In practice, the conflicts have to do mainly with the means of effecting real improvement in the living conditions of the least advantaged, the precise extent of the rights that can be granted to all."[11]

Four points to emphasize here: First, Piketty's political philosophy of equal rights is fundamentally at odds with a caste society—and with the patrimonial capitalism that embodies caste principles. In a caste society, where people are viewed as divided by God or "essence" into fundamentally different orders of being, there is no rhyme or reason to equal rights. Rights, as in the Middle Ages, are parceled out by caste, with the inferior caste not entitled to rights reserved for the aristocracy or castes of higher "essence" or blood. Equal rights require the end of a caste society, and the underlying caste premises that people are designed by God or nature to be unequal in their essences. Castes presume a form of human inequality that cannot be tampered with, and that cannot lead to equal rights for fundamentally different breeds of humans.

Second, following the first point, is that putting into place any serious equal rights philosophy will require abolishing patrimonial capitalism. This, in turn, requires significant redistribution of wealth and greater democratic ownership and control of capital. This is because the extreme concentration of wealth in the patrimonial system prevents the disinherited majority—the lower majoritarian caste class—from gaining access to the capital or wealth that can be used to ensure its rights.

Third, the politics necessary to achieve any kind of more expansive rights regime will have to be driven by democratic movements, led by the disinherited majority. The 1% will resist an expansive interpretation of the equal rights regime. The politics of rights requires a robust democratic mobilization—not the revolutions, Piketty thinks, of the French or American form, but new expansive democratic politics that can overcome the power of ruling caste classes and of dynastic and inherited fortunes.

Fourth, the democratization of capital will help underwrite the social state but is not necessarily a call for a larger government or state ownership. Piketty argues that the twenty-first century will have to be a cauldron of experimental and innovative approaches to spreading wealth and expanding democratic control of capital. This will involve "new decentralized and participatory forms of organization ... along with innovative types of governance, so that a much larger public sector than exists today can be operated efficiently."[12] In other words, Piketty is calling for far more expansive democratic control of capital, but not necessarily in the form of a far greater state. Nonetheless, it is clear that he views growing, innovative forms of democratic control of capital— in other words, systems of economic democracy—as the only way to weaken patrimonial capitalism and its unacceptable denial of rights to the disinherited majority.[13]

What then are the forms of democratic control of capital that are possible, which do not take us to an autocratic, all-consuming state but enable dispossessed caste classes to claim power and rights? Piketty lays out a series of policies and institutional changes that are just the beginning of a conversation about how to democratize capital in the twenty-first century.

The top of Piketty's list is tax policy, especially the global wealth tax widely viewed as his major proposal. There is no question that Piketty views taxes as the most important tool a democracy has to determine its collective future and underwrite a regime of equal rights. One of his most important assertions, worth repeating here, is that "taxation is not a technical matter. It is preeminently a political and philosophical issue, perhaps the most important of all political issues. Without taxes, society has no common destiny and collective action is impossible."[14]

He continues: "How can sovereign citizens democratically decide how much of their resources they wish to devote to common goals, such as education, health, retirement, inequality reduction, employment sustainable development, and so on. Precisely what concrete form taxes take is therefore the crux of political conflict in any society."[15] Tax policy is his foundation for economic democracy, that is, the spreading of control over capital to the disinherited majority, so that they can fashion a decent collective life for all. Taxes are the indispensible approach to achieve both economic and political democracy, all in the service of his philosophy of equal rights.

Piketty is worth reading just for his history of income, estate, and wealth taxes in western Europe and the United States. As noted earlier, despite fevered opposition to taxes in American conservative circles, the United States and Britain have been leaders in progressive, even confiscatory, taxation on the wealthy. Noting that the highest income tax bracket on the rich in the United States averaged 81 percent between 1932 and 1980, Piketty shows that steeply progressive taxes played a major role in reducing inequality during this period.[16] It was during this era that a social state under FDR and LBJ gained a foothold in American life, guaranteeing rights to health care through Medicare, to education through better desegregated public schools, and pensions through Social Security. Mobilization of left-liberal coalitions for steeply progressive taxes was part and parcel of the fight for a new social state and an equal rights regime that took form in the United States in the New Deal and the Great Society.

Piketty emphasizes the importance of wealth taxes as the most important way to attack wealth concentration.[17] Progressive wealth taxes with high rates on the biggest dynastic fortunes—those worth hundreds of millions or billions of dollars—will produce an enormous redistribution of wealth.[18] But they will also create financial transparency, by necessitating a system for disclosure of wealth, especially corporate and great personal wealth, all over the world. Piketty repeatedly emphasizes that locating wealth globally is crucially important for gaining democratic control of capital, regulating financial markets, and protecting democracy itself.[19] Trillions of dollars are currently hidden in offshore havens or trusts or other arcane depositories of the rich. Forcing transparency of this "dark money" would allow us to calculate the true volume of wealth in the world, and provide a rational basis for thinking about how much redistribution we need. Its transparency would enable a system of democratic regulation of global capital that is essential to both preventing new financial crises and protecting democracy itself from a takeover by patrimonial elites who have disguised the true extent of their inherited wealth and the ways they use it to control politics. Piketty says, "The capital tax must first promote democratic and financial transparency: there should be clarity about who owns what assets around the world."[20] The virtues in the United States are obvious, as we look at the amount of "dark money" poured into politics by tycoons like the Koch brothers, willing to spend much of their fortune to get control over Congress and the White House.

Progressive taxation, in sum, creates democratic control of capital by redistributing wealth from the 1% to the state itself, which can then redistribute that wealth to secure for the disinherited majority rights to education, health, and social security. This promotes, of course, a kind of democratic control of capital, but it is not the Marxist variety focused on public or state control of business or the means of production.

Nonetheless, Piketty has put the idea of democratic control of capital back on the table—and his wealth tax proposal has already stirred a lot of discussion. He shows that even a modest wealth tax in Europe and the United States would reduce inequality and help finance the social state. Piketty sees public spending as a leading way to achieve a measure of democratic control over capital. In an argument that is likely to attract people wary of increasing the size of government, he argues that "the fact that a service is publicly financed does not mean that it is produced by people directly employed by the state or other public entities. In education and health, services are provided by many kinds of organizations, including foundations and associations, which are in fact intermediate forms between the state and private enterprise."[21] He continues, "It is perfectly possible that such intermediary forms will become more common in the future, where profit-making corporations already face serious competition and concerns about potential conflicts of interest."[22]

This hardly sounds radical—and it raises some problems. Foundations are typically established by wealthy families—and are controlled by the 1%. Those founded by Rockefeller, Carnegie, Ford, and William Gates, for example, espouse elevated goals of improving education, funding a "green revolution" to alleviate poverty and global warming, and other noble goals; but their "solutions" generally tend to support charter schools, corporate monocrop agriculture, and other 1% corporate aims that do not promote the general interest.[23]

The very strong corporate influence on the state itself, of course, points to problems with the transformative capacity of the "social state" itself. Within a capitalist framework, it is extremely difficult to pursue the expansive equal rights regime that Piketty advocates. In the next chapter, I turn to the question of what that implies for social movements and the politics of achieving democratic control of capital and a society of substantive equal rights.

Piketty should be credited, though, for pointing, if not beyond capitalism, toward new ways of democratizing capital through different models of ownership that involve new balances of public and private control of capital. This takes us into the details of tax policy but also beyond the subject of wealth taxes that has dominated the conversation so far. Piketty's wealth tax is just one foundation of his larger concern with democratizing capital ownership. He notes that "the notion of private property can vary from country to country. . . . There is no single variety of capitalism or organization of production in the developed world today: we live in a mixed economy. . . . This will continue to be true in the future, no doubt more than ever: new forms of organization and ownership remain to be invented."[24]

This gives some clarity to what Piketty means when he says he was born of a generation after the Cold War, which is not bound by old debates about socialism and capitalism. What is clear—and this is key to the conversation that his work should inspire—is that democratic control of capital is the heart of his agenda, and that wealth taxes have to be part of that agenda, but hardly the only part and not tied necessarily to expansive state ownership. In the twenty-first century, how democratic capital control is organized is no longer fixed by an ironclad formula of state ownership or any particular balance of state and nonstate actors. Piketty is probably correct in arguing that that balance will be negotiated differently in different countries and that globally, in the twenty-first century, different nations and progressive coalitions must play out every possible innovative scenario for transferring wealth and control of capital to the disinherited majority, whether it is administered through the state or not.[25]

This is not to say that Piketty dismisses public ownership through the state. When I asked him whether he saw virtues to public ownership, he responded, "Yes. Public ownership of capital assets has proved to be the adequate mode of organization in many sectors with publicly provided services, such as education and health." But he also emphasized the importance of public ownership linked in novel ways with nonstate institutions: "I also see virtues in forms of ownerships that are intermediate between public and private, and that involve new forms of participatory governance, particularly in culture and the medias."

Piketty made clear that he is supportive of many ways to redistribute wealth and increase democratic control of capital. When I asked him if he saw virtues to worker ownership, he said: "Yes. This is one way to spread the private ownership of capital." It is interesting that he sees co-ops as forms of private ownership, making clear he is basically focused on the spread of capital ownership rights throughout the population, whether or not it is linked to the state per se.

Piketty added another comment to my question on worker ownership. He said, "I also believe in worker involvement in decision making irrespective of any capital stake, such as Germany." Piketty is referring here to the codetermination system that developed in Germany after World War II, that legally requires all German companies with five hundred or more employees to have 50 percent of their board of directors elected by workers, regardless of whether the workers own any shares of stock. Seats on the board are a form of ownership rights, involving control of capital even if they don't derive from stock ownership. Codetermination is not revolutionary, but it does involve parceling out the rights of capital ownership to those who don't necessarily own capital. This can be seen as another innovative approach to democratic control of capital, and a form Critical Marxists might consider favorably, because it gives meaningful control over production to workers who are not investors.[26]

Extending that idea to all companies in the United States—along with co-ops or fully worker-owned firms—moves us beyond traditional concepts of capitalism and opens the door to a much more democratically distributed set of ownership rights. Worker pension funds already constitute a dominant or very significant share of total capital in many major firms, another path toward worker ownership that should not be seen as an inconsequential step toward democratic control of capital and economic democracy, though current laws limit worker voting rights on much of their pension capital. In his documentary arguing to replace capitalism, *Capitalism: A Love Story*, filmmaker Michael Moore makes worker ownership his alternative to current capitalism, an idea championed as well by many unions and community organizers working to promote worker and community ownership from Chicago to Cleveland to Boston. "New economy" thinkers in the United States, such as political economist Gar Alperovitz, document the growth and varieties of cooperative economies and worker ownership that are consistent with Piketty's notion of new ways of democratizing capital.[27]

The conversation after Piketty should thus be about wealth taxes, but it is really a larger conversation about democratic control of capital. Piketty has simply opened the door to the necessity of spreading wealth and democratic capital control, without committing to any particular institutional model, beyond a large social state supporting an equal rights regime. He seems to lean toward an expansive model of rights and a concept of democratic capital control that are flexible but that guarantee more democracy and equality, both in the economy and in politics.

Commentators have largely ignored how much of a champion of democracy Piketty is. His focus on inequality is clearly animated by the concern that patrimonial capitalism can easily erode democracy and create autocracy or plutocracy. It is also clear that he sees economic democracy—conceived as democratic control of capital—as the foundation of political democracy. Beyond the current conversation about the wealth tax per se lies a much broader discussion that we have needed in America for a very long time: whether democracy in the nation and the world is doomed if we don't have economic democracy.

Discussion Questions

1. Do you support the idea of a global wealth tax? What would it accomplish?
2. Do you think that Piketty puts too much emphasis on taxes as a way to reduce inequality and democratize capital and wealth?
3. What does Piketty really mean when he talks about "democratic control of capital"?
4. Do you support the democratization of capital?
5. Do you think a majority of Americans support the idea?
6. How do you see the difference between the social state and socialism?

7. Do you believe economic democracy is necessary for political democracy?

8. Do you believe in the "equal rights" doctrine that Piketty espouses? How does it differ from a society of "equal opportunity"?

♦ ♦ ♦

THOMAS PIKETTY AND WEALTH TAXATION IN AMERICA

CHUCK COLLINS AND JOSH HOXIE,
INSTITUTE FOR POLICY STUDIES

> *Every day, members of the top one-thousandth of Americans visit the conference rooms of their high-priced tax attorneys to sign documents that will place their vast fortunes beyond the reach of our estate tax law for the next century or more. These fortunes will sit in giant "dynasty trusts," providing a privileged life for the descendants of today's plutocrats and, in all likelihood, will grow ever larger with each passing generation.*
>
> —Bob Lord, tax attorney, Phoenix, Arizona

The Piketty Moment and the Future of Inequality

One important implication of Thomas Piketty's arguments for US readers is that we should strengthen our estate tax—our nation's only levy on inherited wealth—as a means to reduce the buildup of concentrated wealth and power.

Piketty suggests that wealth inequality is very likely at its highest point in US history, and there is no reason to believe wealth concentration will stop growing on its own. The concentration of wealth is more extreme than we imagined.

The accumulation of wealth of the top 1% over the past thirty years is substantial, but the most dizzying concentration of wealth is among the top one-tenth of the 1%. For example, the four hundred richest Americans, with combined assets of over $2 trillion, now have as much wealth as all 41 million African Americans in the United States.[1]

Piketty, using income tax data dating back centuries, upended the widely held assumption that markets will somehow self-correct widespread inequality. If left unchecked, those who earn their income through investments will continue to see their share of the economy grow steadily while wages continue to stagnate.[2]

Declining Social Mobility

Inequality matters. One of the disastrous results of growing income and wealth polarization is the decline of social mobility. The growth of inequality is having a negative effect on the rising generation.

The United States was once the envy of the world in economic mobility and still prides itself as a socially mobile society where what you do is more important than the racial and class circumstances of your birth. However, European nations and Canada, with their social safety nets and investments in early childhood education, are now experiencing greater social mobility. Emerging sociological research about children and opportunity in the United States indicates that once inequalities open up, they rarely decrease over time.[3] Canada now has three times the social mobility of the United States. [4]

In the three decades after World War II, between 1947 and 1977, social mobility increased, particularly for the white working class.[5] This imprinted a national self-identity as a meritocratic society, especially juxtaposed with the old "caste societies" of Europe, with their static class systems and relatively calcified social mobility.

The idea that people's futures might be economically determined deeply offends US sensibilities. We want to believe that individual moxie matters, that a person's creativity, effort, and intelligence will lead to economic success. Stories of exceptional strivers, heroically overcoming a stacked deck of obstacles, divert our attention from the data. But the large megatrends are now indisputable.

Sustained public investments in opportunity are critical to level a playing field that is constantly being upended by wealth advantage. Unfortunately, at a time when public investment could ensure prosperity for future generations, domestic spending at the state and federal levels has been dramatically reduced.

Emerging Wealth Dynasties and Taxing Inheritances

At the same time that social mobility is declining, one group stands to inherit fantastic sums of money, fueling growing unequal opportunity.

According to Piketty, wealth will continue to concentrate in the hands of a few in the coming decades and have a corrosive impact on our democratic institutions.

A new generation of wealth dynasties is emerging, similar to what our nation witnessed a century ago during the first Gilded Age of 1890–1915. Imagine twenty years from now, a country whose politics and culture is dominated by the offspring of families with names like Walton, Gates, Soros, Adelson, Buffett, and Koch.

An estimated $59 trillion will pass from older generations to younger ones through inheritances over the next fifty-five years. This is estimated to be the largest intergenerational wealth transfer in history.[6]

Piketty calls for wealth taxation as the most important intervention to slow the creation of hereditary wealthy dynasties. He advocates a global tax on wealth to put a brake on the buildup of wealth dynasties.

Taxes, according to Piketty, go to the heart of reducing extreme wealth inequality. "Without taxes," he writes, "society has no common destiny, and collective action is impossible."

In a US context, the federal estate tax is our only meaningful levy on the inherited wealth of multimillionaires and billionaires. It is only paid by households with over $10 million in wealth. Yet at the moment of Piketty's warning, our US estate tax has been deeply weakened by loopholes. Attorneys and tax planners, working on behalf of our nation's wealthiest families, have designed a complex web of trusts that enable these wealth-holders to dodge their responsibilities.

Wealth Taxation in the United States: A Brief History

The estate tax is America's only levy on substantial wealth. Sometimes called the "inheritance tax" or "death tax," the estate tax requires the wealthy to pay a levy on wealth they leave their heirs, after a substantial exemption. Instituted in 1916, the federal estate tax has multiple purposes: (1) raise revenue from those with the greatest capacity to pay; (2) encourage charitable giving and dispersal of wealth; and (3) put a brake on the concentration of wealth and power, with its threat to democracy and social stability.[7]

Like Thomas Piketty, the proponents of an estate tax—ranging from President Theodore Roosevelt to populist farm organizations—viewed the extreme concentrations of wealth during the first Gilded Age, 1890–1915, as a threat to our self-governing democracy. Over the past century, the estate tax has served its stated purpose. When protected from loopholes, the US estate tax raised substantial revenue from those with the greatest capacity to pay. Most important, it ensured that during the years 1930 to 1975, the creation of wealth dynasties was thwarted.

In the 1990s a right-wing movement organized to eliminate the "death tax." In June 2001 the tax was weakened but not eliminated. The present rules governing the estate tax were passed in January 2013 as part of the American Taxpayer Relief Act (ATRA). In 2014 the federal tax is levied on estates with assets (cash, real estate, stocks, or other assets) exceeding $5.34 million (or effectively $10.68 million per married couple). Fewer than 2 out of every 1,000 estates in 2014 will owe estate tax. The tax rate on estate values above the exemption level is fixed at a flat 40 percent, the lowest rate since the 1930s.[8]

Estate Tax Avoidance: The Urgent Need for a Fix

Wealthy families have historically employed estate planners to reduce their estate taxes. But in recent years, the aggressive use of trusts has made the estate tax even more porous. The *Bloomberg News* reported in December 2013 that billionaire casino mogul Sheldon Adelson exploited a trust provision to pass nearly $8 billion to family members and avoid $2.8 billion in estate taxes. The Walton family pioneered the use of these "billionaire loopholes" to place billions outside the reach of taxation for generations to come.[9]

Each day that Congress fails to close these "billionaire loopholes," millions of dollars of wealth are being placed for decades outside of the reach of the estate tax. Without a robust estate tax, Thomas Piketty's nightmare vision of growing concentrations of hereditary wealth will come to pass.

US lawmakers should act immediately to close the "billionaire loophole" as a mechanism for estate and gift tax avoidance and institute other fixes. President Obama has included a proposal to partially fix the problem in each of his annual budgets but has not used any political capital to press it.[10]

Reducing Student Debt with an Opportunity Fund

Promoting progressive estate taxes in isolation has limited public support. Advocates of estate tax repeal have spent millions to save billions for wealthy families, in part by confusing the public over who actually pays the estate tax.[11]

One way to protect the estate tax is to link the revenue to an expenditure that increases opportunity. One plan, articulated by Bill Gates Sr., would create an "education trust fund"—capitalized by a progressive estate tax—that would provide college tuition grants for young people who complete civilian or military service. Gates called this a "G.I. Bill for the next generation."[12] Another option would be to dedicate funds to support early childhood education or the creation of universal asset-savings accounts, so-called baby bonds.

The debt load young people are taking on just to go to college today is staggering. Federal student debt now tops a trillion dollars, more than any time in history and more than credit card debt.[13] A full 40 million Americans hold federal student loans, a figure growing rapidly as nearly three-quarters of the class of 2012 took out student loans, averaging nearly $30,000 per student.[14] This burden is not just relegated to young people, as many parents and other family members are taking on student loans for their children, and many others are still struggling to pay their student loans more than a decade after they attended college. One in five households owed student debt in 2010, with an average student loan balance of nearly $27,000.[15]

The negative impacts of the student debt burden on the younger generation and the overall economy are numerous. A 2007 Princeton University study showed that students graduating with student debt were more likely to choose high-salary jobs and to avoid lower-salary public-interest or mission-based work.[16] A 2014 report has shown that increased student loans are significantly linked to reduced entrepreneurship and small business formation.[17] Growing research has also shown that increasing student debt leads graduates to delays in marriage[18] and homeownership.[19]

The rise in student debt is directly linked to reduced public investment in higher education, which has steadily decreased since 1980 despite a major rise in demand for higher education.[20] Budget cuts at all levels of government have dismantled post–World War II public investments that had begun to level the playing field for economically and racially disadvantaged families.

Higher education has taken one of the biggest hits. State cuts in higher education since 2008 have reduced spending 28 percent per student, a problem as state and local revenues cover 53 percent of college costs. This has led to cuts that jeopardize the quality of education and to tuition hikes averaging 27 percent, with California and Arizona raising tuition over 70 percent. Over the past twenty years, the College Board reports that the cost of four-year college has accelerated faster than median income, even after factoring in federal financial aid and tax subsidies. [21]

Reducing Inequality for the Next Generation

College education continues to play a significant role in employment opportunity and lifetime earnings. A 2010 Georgetown University study projects that nearly two-thirds of jobs will require at least some postsecondary education by 2018.[22] College education is also associated with higher voter registration, volunteerism, and civic engagement.[23]

In the seventy years since World War II, college entry increased by over 50 percent, and the rate of college completion by age twenty-five quadrupled. But since 1980, an income-based gap has grown in terms of college completion.[24] Children from high-income families are much more likely to attend college and much more likely to apply to as well as attend the top-ranked universities. Only 34 percent of high-achieving high school seniors in the bottom fourth of income distribution attend any one of the country's 238 most selective colleges. Among top students in the highest income quartile, that figure is 78 percent.[25]

Young people today have come of age during a time of stagnant wages, especially at the lower income levels typically associated with entry-level jobs. The purchasing power of minimum-wage jobs is lower today than it was in 1968.[26] Median household income in 2010 was just 2.1 percent higher than in 1990. In that same timeframe tuition at four-year colleges skyrocketed to the tune of 112 percent while state investment in higher education dropped by 26 percent.[27] Every state in the nation save one, North Dakota, has continued to reduce higher education funding, with cuts averaging 25 percent per student since 2008.[28] The cost of educating the next generation of workers has shifted dramatically from the public to the individual.

An "education opportunity fund," capitalized by revenue from a progressive estate tax, with funds dedicated to reducing or eliminating college student debt, could reverse these troubling trends. An example of this exists in the state of Washington, where state-level estate tax revenue capitalizes an "education legacy trust fund." The Washington state estate tax withstood a ballot initiative challenge in 2006 in large part because its revenue was dedicated to education.[29]

Conclusion

An important implication of Piketty's work, in the US context, is to protect the estate tax and close the "billionaire loopholes" that are undermining the estate tax. Without a robust estate tax, we will be living under a new generation of plutocratic rule.

Building popular support for taxing inherited fortunes could be accomplished by linking revenue to a popular "opportunity fund," to provide access to high-quality higher education to all Americans, regardless of their ability to pay. This initiative would reduce the crippling student debt today's students are forced to take on to attend college.

Capital in the Twenty-First Century ends on a hopeful note: inequality is growing, but it doesn't have to. Piketty points to the tax code as a mechanism for checking the concentration of wealth. A robust tax on the intergenerational transfer of immense wealth funding an opportunity education trust fund would check the rise of inequality and foster a more level playing field. It would constitute a major investment in the next generation, similar to the investments in the mid-twentieth-century's "Greatest Generation" that led to the creation of the American middle class. It would also capture the imagination of the next generation, whose lives have been marked by the steady public disinvestment from programs of social uplift.

14

♦ ♦ ♦

THE NEW POLITICS

What are the prospects for meaningful change—in inequality and patrimonial capitalism—through electoral politics and social movements? What forms of national politics might the Piketty analysis help create—and is his economic and political analysis bold enough to help create systemic changes in capitalism and fuel political parties or politicians who might be champions of the disinherited majority? Is the Piketty analysis, which embraces capitalism, likely to energize new social movements for equality and social justice, movements that see a need for deeper changes in the economic and political system? Might there be a new movement melding the caste concerns of "identity politics" (e.g., feminism and civil rights) with the class concerns of the minimum-wage worker and the larger disinherited majority? Might there be new forms of the Occupy Wall Street movement to challenge the 1%, with strong support from unions led by women and minorities who see their issues now from a "caste class" perspective? Are we likely to see forceful change from new coalitions of unions, environmentalists, feminists, and civil rights groups, who see economic justice and taking back the country from the 1% as their shared democratic goal?

I saw and met Thomas Piketty on May 31, 2014, at a forum at the historic Old South Meeting House Boston, where he teamed up with Massachusetts Democratic senator Elizabeth Warren, who had just published a best-selling book of her own.[1] Warren is one of the champions of the progressive base of the Democratic Party, based on her relentless attacks on the Wall Street 1%, and its clear and present threat to social justice and democracy. In the Boston forum, Piketty, a modest and disarming intellectual, summarized the key points of his book, from his views of extreme inequality to the case for a global wealth tax. Warren then took the stage and essentially laid out a progressive agenda for America that seemed in large measure to draw from Piketty's vision of patrimonial capitalism. She discussed the dangers of extreme inequality, the suffering experienced by the disinherited majority, and the threats to democracy that concentrated wealth now posed to the nation and the world.

Piketty smiled through much of Warren's charismatic advocacy of a Left populism. It is an American politics seeking to regain democratic control of the nation's wealth from Wall Street and the 1%. Warren pulled no punches; she detailed graphically all the ways in which the largest Wall Street banks and other American corporations, as well as the wealthiest of American families, were destroying the American Dream, dismantling most of the opportunities for the disinherited majority to live a decent life that the New Deal had begun to create for their parents and grandparents. She pointed out that students were over $1 trillion in debt through often fraudulent student loans; millions of homeowners were still underwater on their mortgages because of Wall Street subprime loans; millions of workers had dropped out of the labor force because jobs were disappearing; millions of minorities and low-income women were falling into a bottomless pit from which they could not climb out; millions of working people, including two-parent families as well as single mothers, faced bankruptcy because of low wages and high debt created by the 1% in doing whatever necessary to increase its wealth.[2]

Senator Warren is championing a politics of class confrontation with the 1%, a theme that is resonating not only with the Democratic Party progressive base but large numbers of other more conservative Americans troubled by the greed and fraud of the biggest banks that drove America into a ditch, and the bailouts that allowed the 1% to escape largely unscathed. Warren wants to hold the big banks responsible, force their leaders to go to jail or pay millions of dollars for their crimes, create an expansive regulatory system to prevent another collapse of the financial system, strengthen the Consumer Finance Protection Bureau that she proposed to protect the public against the 1% from exploitative Wall Street loans and credit deals, and tax the wealthy to help provide for the mass of low-income workers and reduce the extreme inequality now threatening democracy in America. She made her reputation as a defender of the disinherited majority against the 1%, and a large number in the Democratic base have supported her, rather than Hillary Clinton, to be the 2016 Democratic Party candidate for president.

In Boston, Piketty and Warren simultaneously autographed each other's books, a symbol of the politics that Piketty's work might help fuel in the United States. In his book, Piketty focuses on the "social state"—a version of the European social democratic or welfare state—and enacting more progressive income and wealth taxes, but he says little about his political strategy to achieve his aims, especially in the United States. Many commentators, such as political economist Robert Kuttner and political analyst Thomas Frank, have critiqued Piketty for his failure to discuss in any depth the critical importance of Franklin Roosevelt, the labor movement, and the New Deal in reversing the inequality and class exploitation of the mid-twentieth-century era.[3] Likewise, Piketty says shockingly little about the central role of the Reagan revolution in reversing the gains of the New Deal and putting in place the twenty-first-century patrimonial capitalism that his book is all about. Given the extreme importance of right-wing movements and Reagan-era policies—in concentrating wealth and returning to extreme inequality—Piketty's failure to discuss it in any depth is one of the important omissions of his book. One could easily conclude that Piketty sees little hope of change through political movements or through electoral politics or state policy.

I have already discussed Piketty's failure to consider in detail both the New Deal and the Reagan revolution, reflecting Piketty 1's more mechanistic and detached traditional economics approach. His lack of an extensive. discussion of US political history and state policy will understandably turn off many American progressives and Leftists, who will not find the political analysis at the heart of many of the problems Piketty himself identifies. In my own reading, I found his American political analysis and history to be sparse. He tends to offer largely reformist political solutions consistent with most academic Keynesian thinking, which shies away from social movements and embraces capitalism. In other words, Piketty's frame of analysis as a Keynesian economist (really Piketty 1) has contributed to the political limitations of his work.

Nonetheless, to conclude that Piketty has no important political vision or sees little role for electoral politics, or for social movements as discussed below, would be a major mistake. First, Piketty spends a good deal more time talking about European, and specifically French, politics—both through nineteenth-century novels and current events—than he does American politics, and the gaping omissions in the discussion of politics and state policy in the United States may reflect his lack of immersion in American political history and his greater comfort zone in discussing European politics. He does, in fact, play a role as an advisor to French social democratic and socialist parties and has been active in European-Union political and regulatory organizations as well. Moreover, he has acknowledged in interviews that he feels he did not give enough attention to the New Deal and the labor movement in explaining the midcentury American era's reversal of Gilded Age capitalism.[4]

Second, Piketty—and this is now Piketty 2—has championed, as discussed in the previous chapter, the social state and a strong regime of equal rights and substantive democracy. Piketty is clear that he is interested in inequality because he sees it as threatening democracy and social justice. His advocacy of the social state, the democratic ownership of capital, and a regime of equal rights (rather than equal opportunity) all point to a political analysis that may not be fully developed in this book but is something that can be used by progressives and even socialists to advocate for more visionary political change.[5]

It would make no sense to say that Piketty sees no role for electoral politics—or social movements—given that he explicitly articulates a political vision that can only be achieved through democratic state policy and democratization of capital. True, the social state is not anything resembling communism or even socialism in the Marxist sense, and many neo-Marxists will see the politics of even Piketty 2 as disappointing. Again, many on the Left will view Piketty 2 as, at best, an innovative Keynesian economist, but one who has embraced capitalism and is focused only on redistributing its fruits. Many will argue that he lacks an original political agenda beyond his global wealth tax proposal.

While Piketty is certainly not rejecting capitalism and is no political visionary, Piketty 2 opens up a frame of analysis that more visionary and activist political thinkers can and should probe. He has shown that the deep inequalities of capitalism reflect markets working perfectly—and that these inequalities threaten democracy. A logical conclusion is that capitalism is largely programmed to replace democracy with plutocracy or autocracy. Moreover, he has effectively critiqued capitalist theories that describe the market as serving the common good and reflecting meritocracy. Piketty shows that pay, especially at the top, reflects more the "hand in the till" than the invisible hand. His central advocacy of democratic ownership of capital can be developed by American progressives to advocate for a new economic system organized around socialist or cooperativist ideas, some of which—such as worker ownership—Piketty embraces. And his central focus on the 1% converges with the many political currents in the United States that now focus on the injustice and antidemocratic elements of America's extreme inequality. Piketty's work could give ammunition and credibility to an American majority seeking major changes on Wall Street and in corporate power and money in politics—changes that can only be accomplished through a new class-based politics organized to regain control of America from the 1%.

This takes us back to Senator Warren and Piketty's appearance with her in Boston. Their joint appearance offers hints of how Piketty's book converges with American electoral politics and social movements that may find fuel for their struggle in his analysis. At minimum, one can say this: first, Piketty sees strong political action as necessary; second, he believes in electoral politics—and a progressive Democratic politics of the kind Warren champions; third, he supports a class politics focused on redistributing the wealth of the 1%; and fourth, considering Warren's attention to the economic needs of women and minorities, Piketty supports the melding of a caste and class politics that might be just the political medicine needed to liberate the nation from the grips of patrimonial capitalism.

Other key questions remain: whether Warren-style politics, which Piketty appears to support, is truly a new class politics far-reaching enough to end the 1%'s control of the nation; whether it is too far-reaching to attract the support of the Democratic Party itself or the majority of the US population; whether any form of electoral politics in patrimonial capitalism can change the system; whether Piketty's analysis can help grassroots social movements, going well beyond current policies of the Democratic Party, to successfully take on the 1%; and whether caste and class can meld in American progressivism, linking feminism, civil rights, and other caste movements with the labor movement in a common "caste class" struggle of the disinherited majority against the 1%.

This last set of questions will determine the political legacy of Piketty's work. Recall that at the outset, I suggested his work could become one of those rare books that help start a new national conversation, fueling new politics and changing the country. Can his book spawn a new discussion and a new movement to replace the rule of the 1% with the rule of the disinherited majority? Would such a movement reflect insights from Piketty's analysis? If so, we need to see whether any such new movement pursues an agenda of equal rights rather than simply equal opportunity and a form of economic democracy that ends patrimonial capitalism and leads to democratic control of capital and the state.

First question: Is the progressive base of the Democratic Party, inspired by leaders such as Senator Warren and Vermont Independent senator Bernie Sanders, offering a new class politics truly oriented to end the rule of the 1%? In my view, both Warren and Sanders—as well as the progressive Democratic base—want to beat back, if not end, the 1%'s control of the United States and create more democratic control by the disinherited majority. Warren's political career has been built attacking the wealth and power of Wall Street, and she has fought against the odds to create a tax system on wealth, a strong Wall Street regulatory regime, a living wage, and an end to the financialized economy and oligarchic politics that the big Wall Street firms have built and now control. Bernie Sanders is an avowed socialist, the only one in the Senate. He also has made extreme inequality, the wealth and greed of Wall Street, the overwhelming role of corporate money in politics, and the disinheritance of the poor and working class the central focus of his political agenda. Moreover, much of the base of the Democratic Party is supportive of the Warren-Sanders approach and views extreme inequality and the control by the 1% as evils that they are fighting to overcome.

Do the progressive Democrats go far enough in articulating a class politics that can actually end the rule of the 1% and create democratic control of capital by the disinherited majority? No. A real class politics would have to go further. It would talk about the need to build a mass populist social movement to transform capitalism and create a new cooperativist economy or economic democracy. It would need to break apart the largest banks or nationalize them, advocate for a transformation of corporate governance toward worker ownership or codetermination, highlight the importance of unions and labor rights—including legal rights for workers to form unions without reprisals and to control their working conditions through worker councils—attack the legitimacy of the entire global structure of patrimonial capitalism that the 1% helped build, support a localized economy with community ownership and limitation of large corporate control over local politics, and push for an end to corporate personhood and creation of a fully publicly funded campaign financing system, overturning Citizens United, McCutcheon, and other Supreme Court decisions that allow billionaires to pour as much money as needed to get their own candidates elected and under their control. It would also champion an expansive social state providing single-payer health care, affordable or free higher education, a more generous Social Security program, and vocational education for the working class; promote social guarantees of minimal income and full employment pulling low-income workers, especially women and minorities, out of poverty; and create a far more progressive tax system including a wealth tax with steeply progressive rates on the highest fortunes. Most important, it would also advocate for massive public investment in green jobs and the creation of a new clean energy infrastructure to stop climate change, as well as an end to US militarism and imperialism.[6] Piketty himself would likely champion many of these policies, and both Warren and Sanders, as well as their supporters, have already advocated for a great many of them as well. Nonetheless, the ones that go furthest in building the social state and democratizing control of capital are the least fully developed and discussed.

Living in Europe, Piketty can embrace some of these policies more easily than American politicians, writers, or voters, because they are already part of the European order. The aforementioned agenda is hardly revolutionary, but it is more expansive than any ever advanced by an American mainstream political party, although the 1892 People's Party, created by populists focused on ending Wall Street's domination of Gilded America, went some distance in this direction, explicitly advocating nationalization of Wall Street banks.[7] The New Deal and the Great Society of the 1960s made steps toward a social state but never advocated the key planks for democratic control of capital or nationalization of the banks and support of worker ownership or control of production. Considering all this, the Warren-Sanders progressive wing of the Democratic Party has probably gone as far as it can in the electoral arena without the support of new social movements that we discuss shortly.

It is also important to remember that the Democratic Party, within the context of patrimonial capitalism, has become dependent on the support of Wall Street and other wealthy benefactors within the 1%. This has long been the case. Political sociologist G. William Domhoff, in influential books like *Who Rules America?*, *The Higher Circles*, and *The Myth of Political Ascendancy*, has documented the control by corporate and wealthy elites of both major parties, including even during the New Deal era when the Democratic Party was subordinated to a liberal corporate coalition aligned with conservative Southern Democrats.[8] The billions of dollars necessary to win the presidency and Congress has, today, made open breaks with the 1% appear suicidal to mainstream party leaders, many of whom long ago made their peace with the 1%, including Bill Clinton and Hillary Clinton. As such, the Warren-Sanders wing and the progressive base are likely the best we can hope for from the Democratic Party, and the base will find it extremely difficult to get party leaders to accept their relatively modest progressive agenda.

Nonetheless, the anger within most supporters of the Democratic Party—and even within the a majority of the entire US population—about extreme inequality, the rigged rules and bailouts of the 1%, and the collapse of the American Dream for the disinherited majority all suggest that the Warren-Sanders wing could find new opportunities for progressive Democrats that resonate with the mood of the country. Much as the Tea Party was able to pull the establishment Republican Party leadership far to the populist Right, the progressive Democrats now have a similar opportunity to press their case and rescue the Democratic Party, under the leadership of Barack Obama or Hillary Clinton, from being the party of Bush Lite.

The prospects of electoral party politics serving the disinherited majority are ultimately dependent on the rise of new grassroots movements—both caste- and class-based—which can push the Democratic Party in a far more progressive direction.[9] America has always been a land of strong grassroots movements for progressive change, as historian Howard Zinn discusses so vividly in his *People's History of the United States*.[10] The prospects for a new class politics targeting the 1% depend ultimately on new social movements rising—especially those that can unite caste and class groups in the struggle against patrimonial capitalism.

Would Piketty himself support such movements? As discussed previously, he offers far too little historical discussion of such movements in his book, and one might come away uncertain about whether he believes in their importance. Keynesian political economists often engage politically not by joining social movements on the streets but by consulting with political leaders about policy prescriptions, and helping create the intellectual climate for a new direction, much as members of Franklin Roosevelt's kitchen cabinet did in the New Deal. In his book, Piketty voices an "optimism" about the "power of ideas" and the ability of intellectuals to influence the decision of parties and political leaders.

And Piketty himself has played that role with social democratic leaders and socialist parties in France and in the EU.

This would seem to suggest that Piketty might be this type of Keynesian, who sees little promise in social movements. Yet, when I asked him specifically whether he supported the Occupy Wall Street movement, he responded with a vigorous "Yes!" Occupy made the 1% the target of its own analysis and activism. Piketty mentions that Occupy successfully introduced the slogan of "we are the 99%" that speaks to the plight of the disinherited majority, and he reasons that social scientists are citizens like everyone else and should take active political stances.[11]

While Occupy is often seen as a failure, it had great success in making the concepts of the 1% and the 99% part of American public discourse. Piketty makes reference to this, and one might well argue that the resonance to his book might not have been possible had not Occupy risen up against the very 1% that is the focus of Piketty's book. More important, it has introduced a language conducive to the development of a serious class politics in the United States.

Moreover, while Piketty is not a Marxist, as I have repeatedly pointed out, he does believe in class analysis and the democratic control of capital, two of the key ideas of not just Marxism but the broader Left tradition in the United States and the world. Because he does not offer a Marxist definition of classes, I asked him specifically whether he believed that classes, as he defined them, had "class interests" and engaged in class conflicts. His answer, as noted earlier: "My 'classes' are continuous and multidimensional, but of course they do have class interests and generate class conflict."

This brings social movements back to center stage. If classes exist and engage in class struggle, then it is the labor movement, and grass-roots movements more broadly, that move to the forefront of politics. The Establishment of the Democratic Party is to a large degree a captive of the 1%. But the Democratic base that helps to make up the labor movement, the environmental and climate movements, the peace movement, and civil rights movements do not have to pay homage to the 1%. Grassroots movements are the vehicles for the Democratic base—and others not affiliated with the Democratic Party—to organize mass popular opposition to the 1% and to bring their own party Establishment into opposition with them.[12]

Piketty's work has highlighted something already brewing just underneath the surface of American consciousness. Class power and concentrated wealth have emerged as the primary enemy of democracy and the American Dream. Only grassroots movements can bring this effort against the 1% into a well-organized class struggle that commands the attention of the Democratic Party and forces it to move against control by the 1%.[13]

Of course, the labor movement has been systematically decimated by the 1%, so all of this might seem academic. Yet Piketty's analysis of patrimonial capitalism brings what may be a saving grace to the prospects for challenging the 1%. First, it offers a rigorously documented analysis that is so vivid about the mal-distribution of wealth and the poison of extreme inequality, programmed to a large degree into the markets themselves, that it could create a new conversation in the general public about the dangers of markets and even capitalism itself, one that taps into preexisting sentiments intensified by the Great Recession. *Capitalism* polls poorly as a word, especially among youth in America. According to a 2010 Pew poll, 43 percent of young Americans say they feel "positive" about socialism, about the same percentage who say they feel positive about capitalism. Among all adult Americans, only 52 percent react positively to the word *capitalism* in the Pew poll, titled "Socialism Not so Negative; Capitalism Not so Positive." In a 2009 Rasmussen poll, only 53 percent of all Americans described capitalism as "superior" to socialism.[14] Second, it shows that the inheritance principle central to patrimonial capitalism has made caste once again a central social reality—not just for women and minorities and gays but also for almost all workers.

The political implications have a great deal to do with the power of caste politics in America—and its potential convergence in the twenty-first century with class politics. The most successful grassroots social movements in America have been the civil rights and women's movements, both of which have argued that inherited qualities such as skin color or gender are an unacceptable and unconstitutional basis for discrimination and inequality. These movements have not eliminated racism or sexism, but they have led to the greatest progressive victories in American history: the end of slavery, the right of women to vote, and the progress of both African Americans and women toward eliminating legal race and sex barriers—that is, caste barriers based on inherited and permanent attributes.

Part of the reason for this success is that capitalism itself claims to create "equal opportunity" for all, independent of birth or caste. Marx himself celebrated capitalism as a progressive force historically, as it challenged the caste-based order of feudalism, in which birth determined one's station for life. Civil rights and feminist groups, as well as gay movements, are caste-based movements. The identity politics they champion is consistent with the claims of capitalism to legitimacy, because it creates a society in which all are free to rise and succeed based on merit. By resonating with capitalist ideology about equal opportunity for all, caste movements have gained remarkable traction in America.

In challenging caste, however, identity politics has not generally identified with class politics or any challenges to the corporate system and the ruling 1%. This has had two major consequences. First, it has seriously weakened progressive class movements, with the labor movement divided by race and gender. Labor struggles often have failed because of these divisions. Second, it has made it impossible for civil rights and feminist movements to address successfully the economic problems—low wages, unemployment, and poverty, to name a few—suffered by the majority of African Americans and women.

In the twenty-first century, the prospects for progressive politics depend on overcoming the division between caste and class social movements. Caste movements need an economic agenda to conquer their most pressing current problems. Class movements need to ally and integrate with caste movements to gain the moral authority and raw political power to challenge the corporate system and the 1%.

Here is where Piketty's analysis offers its greatest intrigue and hope for social justice activists. In patrimonial capitalism, inheritance becomes not just a defining principle of groups such as African Americans and women, but of the economic system and society as a whole. As the wealth of the nation becomes concentrated in the dynastic fortunes of the 1% and their children, inherited wealth becomes the principal basis for success. All those without such inherited wealth—that is, the disinherited majority—become not only disadvantaged economic classes but subordinated castes, with little opportunity to advance, whatever their merit. We thus have "caste classes" that, for the disinherited majority, unite subordinated class and caste forms of being.

As discussed already, patrimonial capitalism creates "caste classes," a tip-top 1% with enormous inherited wealth, and a bottom, disinherited

50 percent majority with virtually no wealth and little mobility. A large percentage of this disinherited majority are people of color or single women, who are now doubly disinherited by virtue of their biology and their economic station. Another large percentage of the disinherited are white working-class men, whose identity as a subordinated class struggling with job insecurity and stagnant wages is now compounded by their position as an economic caste, destined to remain excluded from wealth and power and lacking any reasonable prospect of moving up toward a dignified life.

These two groups—low-income biologically defined castes and poor or working-class white men—have historically been pitted against each other.[15] But in patrimonial capitalism, the forces that divide them may become weaker than the forces uniting them. Both are now facing the condition that capitalism claimed to abolish: inheritance of a caste station for life. But both now share precisely that condition, condemned to a lower caste (and class) station in perpetuity.

Inheritance and disinheritance thus become the poles that logically define the politics of a twenty-first-century patrimonial capitalism, in which a very rich dynastic 1% commands overwhelming wealth and political power. Piketty's greatest originality is in making clear that such class control is not based on merit or hard work, but rather, increasingly, on inherited wealth. He also makes clear that the dispossession of the majority is inherited and is not a reflection of its merit or worth.

This is where the realities of the patrimonial capitalist order collides with its own myths. The triumph of inheritance over meritocracy has the potential to expose the illusions of the American Dream and subvert the legitimacy of capitalism itself. If people lose faith in hard work, and believe that birth and inheritance now rule, the American Dream might increasingly seem to more and more Americans a fairy tale with no credibility. And if people believe that capitalism itself is not meritocratic and does not reward talent or hard work—but rather rewards inherited privilege and wealth—then belief in capitalism itself could collapse like a house of cards.

We do not yet know whether caste and class movements will begin to unite and fight together against the principle of inherited wealth and the control of the 1%, which is class rule based on inheritance. Nonetheless, there are signs it is possible. The language of the 1% and the 99% introduced by Occupy has gained a standing in everyday life. The disinherited majority is angry about the power of concentrated wealth and increasingly identifies capitalism as class rule by corporations and billionaires. The 1% is showing its colors as a class born on third base rather than hitting a home run.

Meanwhile, the political stirrings of the disinherited majority, symbolized most vividly at this writing in late 2014 by the McDonald's and Walmart low-wage workers fighting for increases in the minimum wage, are defining themselves as a "civil rights" movement. This no doubt partly reflects the disproportionate share of these workers who are people of color and single mothers. It also may be a sign of the self-conscious rise of a caste class movement that is using caste language to bolster its class struggles. Low-wage service workers, who know the biology of caste discrimination, now are recognizing that their class position has also become a caste, a fixed station for life. The "double-caste" status of the disinherited majority could create a powerful political brew, leading to larger cultural and political changes that begin to break down traditional divisions between white male workers and people of color or single mothers.

There is no certainty that biological caste and economic caste will create a new political alignment or a rejuvenated labor or populist progressive movement. White male workers reduced for life to low economic caste status might become yet more antagonistic to women or people of color, since biological caste privilege might become their only saving grace. Moreover, the enormous control of the media by the wealthy will create intense ideological programming to convince people that merit still matters and that anyone who works hard can make it. Unions have been decimated, and it is unclear that a melding of caste and class movements can revive them.

Nonetheless, the promise of a progressive new political alignment is real, both in the form of revived social movements and the expansion of the progressive Democratic Party popular base. Their own life condition and thinking are more closely wedded to the conditions and ideology of the general population than the 1%, who live on their own luxury planet. Piketty has argued that everything in politics is contingent, and this is certainly true of future prospects of "caste class" movements. Moreover, Piketty himself has offered little political analysis and strategy to suggest how such new movements could form and gain traction in the political arena. Nonetheless, his analysis offers a new basis of hope, and it is one we should not forget or squander.

Discussion Questions

1. Do you believe that Piketty's book is tapping into a growing anger toward the 1% and a discontent even with capitalism itself?
2. Do you see an alignment between Piketty's politics and the politics of the progressive wing of the Democratic Party?
3. What do you see as the likely political reaction to the growth of extreme inequality?
4. Do you think Americans will respond negatively to the inherited wealth of the 1% and the growing importance of the inheritance principle in American society?
5. Do most Americans, in your view, still believe that hard work and merit lead to success in America? Might Piketty's findings make Americans question this assumption?
6. Do you feel that most working Americans feel more like a caste, stuck for life in their economic station?
7. Can you see caste and class politics—the civil rights and feminist movements—joining forces with the working class and white male workers to challenge the 1%?
8. Do you have hope for new social movements that can challenge the 1%?
9. What did you think of Occupy Wall Street, and do you think the movement could be a forerunner of the new politics confronting the 1%?
10. Are you hopeful that we can end patrimonial capitalism and create politics ensuring a more just economic and political system?

♦ ♦ ♦

INTERVIEW WITH THOMAS PIKETTY

Do your "classes" have "class interests"? If so, do they imply class conflict?

My "classes" are continuous and multidimensional, but of course they do have class interests and general class conflict.

Do you see virtues to worker ownership?

Yes. This is one way to spread the private ownership of capital. I also believe in worker involvement in decision making irrespective of any capital stake, such as Germany.

Do you see virtues to public ownership?

Yes. Public ownership of capital assets has proved to be the adequate mode of organization in many sectors with publicly provided services, such as education and health. I also see virtues in forms of ownerships that are intermediate between public and private, and that involve new forms of participatory governance, particularly in culture and the medias.

Do you see an important role for grassroots movements like Occupy?

Yes!

Why have Anglo-American nations been more receptive to progressive income and wealth taxes than the Continental nations?

Part of the explanation is that in Continental Europe, a very significant part of wealth redistribution was in effect achieved through war destructions, so there was less of a need for steeply progressive taxation. Generally speaking, I do not believe in deep national identities: each country has its own national history and set of beliefs and attitudes with respect to money and inequality, but these national trajectories are not deterministic; they are influenced by external shocks and by one another.

Is the rate of growth necessary for more equality environmentally sustainable?

With the current technology, growth is not sustainable for very long. In theory it is possible to invent clean energy sources and have permanent immaterial growth, but we do not have these technologies yet. In any case, this won't solve $r > g$.

Justice Brandeis said, "You can have great wealth and you can have democracy, but you can't have both." Do you agree?

I would put it differently: capitalism can be the slave of democracy, or the opposite, but one has to choose.

NOTES

Notes to Preface

1. Thomas Piketty, *Capital in the Twenty-First Century* (Cambridge, MA: Belknap, 2014).

Notes to Introduction

1. For a discussion of caste from the perspective of political economy, see Charles Derber and Yale Magrass, *Capitalism: Should You Buy It? An Invitation to Political Economy* (Boulder, CO: Paradigm, 2014), 217–218.

2. Thomas Piketty, *Capital in the Twenty-First Century* (Cambridge, MA: Belknap, 2014), 27.

3. Ibid.

4. Ibid., 13ff.

5. Marx gets priority. Piketty discusses him beginning on p. 7 for several pages and then returns to Marx many times in the text. It has been a long time since mainstream economists have treated Marx as a serious thinker, or even mentioned him. Ibid., 7–11.

6. Ibid., 16.

7. Ibid., 39.

8. Ibid., 41.

9. Ibid., 48.

10. Ibid.

11. Ibid.

12. Ibid., 43.

13. Ibid., 52.

14. Ibid., 52.

15. Ibid., 234.

16. Ibid.

17. Ibid., 438.

18. Ibid., 314.

19. Ibid., 333.

20. Ibid., 349.

21. Ibid., 351.

22. Ibid., 353.

23. Ibid.

24. Ibid., 26.

25. Ibid., 402, 428.

26. Ibid., 403.

27. Ibid., 493.

28. Ibid.

Notes to Chapter 1

1. James K. Galbraith, "*Kapital* for the Twenty-First Century?" *Dissent*, Spring 2014, http://www.dissentmagazine.org/article/kapital-for-the-twenty-first-century.

2. Paul Krugman, "Why We're in a New Gilded Age," *New York Review of Books*, May 8, 2014, http://www.nybooks.com/articles/archives/2014/may/08/thomas-piketty-new-gilded-age/.

3. Alvin Gouldner, *The Two Marxisms* (New York: Oxford University Press, 1964).

4. Betty Friedan, *The Feminine Mystique: Fiftieth Anniversary Edition* (New York: W.W. Norton, 2013); Michael Harrington, *The Other America: Poverty in the United States* (New York: Scribner, 1997 reprint); Rachel Carson, *Silent Spring* (Boston: Houghton Mifflin, 2002 reprint).

5. Alexander Kaufman, "Pope Francis: 'Inequality Is the Root of Social Evil,'" *Huffington Post*, April 28, 2014, http://www.huffingtonpost.com/2014/04/28/pope-francis-tweet-inequality_n_5227563.html.

Notes to Chapter 2

1. Thomas Piketty, *Capital in the Twenty-First Century* (Cambridge, MA: Belknap, 2014), 31.

2. Ibid., 32.

3. Ibid.

4. Charles Derber and Yale Magrass, *Capitalism: Should You Buy It? An Invitation to Political Economy* (Boulder, CO: Paradigm, 2014), chapters 1–2.

5. Ibid.

6. Piketty, *Capital*, 32–33.

7. See Paul Krugman, "How Did Economists Get It So Wrong?," *New York Times*, September 6, 2009.

8. Robert Kuttner, "The Poverty of Economics," *Atlantic*, February 1985, 74–84.

9. Piketty, *Capital*, 33.

10. Ibid.

11. Derber and Magrass, *Capitalism*.

Notes to Chapter 3

1. Thomas Piketty, *Capital in the Twenty-First Century* (Cambridge, MA: Belknap, 2014), 250–252.

2. Ibid., 252.

3. Ibid.

4. Ibid.

5. Ibid., 254.

6. See my book *Marx's Ghost: Midnight Conversations on Changing the World* (Boulder, CO: Paradigm, 2011). See also Charles Derber and Yale Magrass, *Capitalism: Should You Buy It? An Invitation to Political Economy* (Boulder, CO: Paradigm, 2014).

7. Piketty, *Capital*, 250–252.

8. Ibid., 251.

9. Ibid., 254.

10. Ibid., 314.

11. This argument is laid out in graphic detail in Part 3 of his book, where Piketty compares the historical and contemporary inequality and class differences between Europe and the United States.

Notes to Chapter 4

1. Thomas Piketty, *Capital in the Twenty-First Century* (Cambridge, MA: Belknap, 2014), 252.

2. Ibid., 250–251.

3. Ibid., 252.

4. Ibid., 250.

5. This is the most obvious difference between Piketty and Marx. Marx's major works detail the historical conflicts between classes whereas Piketty says almost nothing about the history of class conflict. This reflects the way in which definitions of class shape analysis and also reflect the intention of the authors. Marx wanted to mobilize the labor movement to overthrow the capitalist class. Piketty embraces capitalism and seeks experts as major movers for change, rather than the working class, although he does acknowledge the contribution of Occupy.

6. See Karl Marx, *The Communist Manifesto*. See also Charles Derber and Yale Magrass, *Capitalism: Should You Buy It? An Invitation to Political Economy* (Boulder, CO: Paradigm, 2014), chapter 5; and Charles Derber, *Marx's Ghost: Midnight Conversations on Changing the World* (Boulder, CO: Paradigm, 2011).

7. The lack of attention to working-class movements in eras like the New Deal—and to the New Deal itself—is a central point of Robert Kuttner's review of Piketty. See Robert Kuttner, "What Piketty Leaves Out," *American Prospect*, April 2014, http://prospect.org/article/what -piketty-leaves-out.

8. Mike Savage, "Sociological Ruminations on Piketty," Stratification and Culture Research Network, July 1, 2014, http://stratificationandculture.wordpress.com/2014/07/01 /sociological-ruminations-on-piketty/.

9. David Harvey, "Afterthoughts on Piketty's Capital," Reading Marx's Capital with David Harvey, May 5, 2014, http://davidharvey.org/2014/05/afterthoughts-pikettys-capital/. See also James K. Galbraith, "*Kapital* for the Twenty-First Century?" *Dissent*, Spring 2014, http://www .dissentmagazine.org/article/kapital-for-the-twenty-first-century.

10. Both Harvey and Galbraith argue that Piketty cannot report a stable value of capital because of the way he defines it. Harvey indicates it is because of the lack of attention to the labor theory of value—the "dead labor," as Marx wrote, that defines all value in capital. Galbraith refers to the volatility in the stock market of stocks and bonds, which means that Piketty's value of capital fluctuates so rapidly and is vulnerable to bubbles and collapses to the point that Piketty cannot arrive at any meaningful definition of the value of capital.

11. Kuttner, "What Piketty Leaves Out."

12. Thomas Frank, *What's the Matter with Kansas? How Conservatives Won the Heart of America* (New York: Holt, 2005).

13. William Domhoff, *Who Rules America? The Triumph of the Corporate Rich*, 7th ed. (New York: McGraw-Hill, 2013).

14. Piketty, *Capital*, 238–242.

15. Ibid., 415ff.

Notes to Chapter 5

1. For a discussion of caste from the perspective of political economy, see Charles Derber and Yale Magrass, *Capitalism: Should You Buy It? An Invitation to Political Economy* (Boulder, CO: Paradigm, 2014).

2. Ibid., 217; see also the entirety of chapter 12 on the political economy of race.

3. Charles Derber, "Piketty's New Class," Truthout, July 14, 2014, http://www.truth-out. org/opinion/item/24651-pikettys-new-class.

4. A number of feminist writers, specifically in addressing Piketty's work, have high-lighted the reality that despite feminist successes, women have been disproportionately harmed by growing wage and wealth inequality. Some decry the lack of commentary by women and minorities about the way in which the condition of women and people of color are impacted. For an initial discussion of this problem, which at least recognizes the vulner-ability of gender and race castes to growing inequality—and implicitly acknowledges that

caste-oriented feminist and civil rights movements have not risen to address this challenge, see Kathleen Geier, Kate Bahn, Joelle Gamble, Zillah Eisenstein, and Heather Boushey, "How Gender Changes Piketty's Analysis of Capital in the Twenty-First Century," *Nation*, July 7, 2014.

5. Derber, "Piketty's New Class."

6. Thomas Piketty, *Capital in the Twenty-First Century* (Cambridge, MA: Belknap, 2014), 484–487.

7. See Chapter 9 on the American Dream. See also ibid., 484–487.

8. Piketty makes this argument in his discussion of meritocracy. It is also developed in Derber and Magrass, *Capitalism*, especially 107–112.

9. William Domhoff, *The Bohemian Groves and Other Retreats* (New York: Harper Collins College Division, 1975).

10. Geier et al., "How Gender Changes Piketty's Analysis of Capital in the Twenty-First Century."

Notes to Chapter 6

1. Karl Marx, *Capital, Volume 1: A Critique of Political Economy* (New York: Penguin Classics, 1992).

2. In *The Communist Manifesto*, Marx supports unions organizing for higher wages but makes clear that the main goal is a revolution to overturn capitalism. See Karl Marx and Frederick Engels, *The Communist Manifesto* (New York: Merlin, 1998 reprint).

3. Russell Jacoby, "Piketty and Marx: Where They Disagree," *New Republic*, July 2014, posted on http://www.newrepublic.com/article/118024/piketty-and-marx-where-they -disagree.

4. Ibid.

5. Joseph Stiglitz, *The Price of Inequality: How Today's Divided Society Endangers Our Future* (New York: W.W. Norton, 2013); Robert Reich, *Aftershock: The Next Economy and America's Future* (New York: Knopf, 2010).

6. Adam Smith, *The Wealth of Nations* (New York: Modern Library Classics, 2000); Milton Friedman, *Capitalism and Freedom*: Fortieth Anniversary Edition (Chicago: University of Chicago Press, 2002); Marx, *Capital*.

7. Smith, *Wealth of Nations*. See also Charles Derber and Yale Magrass, *Capitalism: Should You Buy It? An Invitation to Political Economy* (Boulder, CO: Paradigm, 2014), chapter 3.

8. Derber and Magrass, *Capitalism*, chapter 3.

9. Ibid.

10. Thomas Piketty, *Capital in the Twenty-First Century* (Cambridge, MA: Belknap, 2014), 308ff.

11. Ibid., 307–308.

12. Ibid., 331.

13. Ibid., 331–332.

14. Ibid., 332.

15. Ibid., 331.

16. Ibid., 333.

17. Ibid., 332.

18. Ibid., 308.

19. Ibid., 308.

20. Ibid., 332.

21. Ibid., 333.

22. Ibid., 332.

23. Ibid., 31–33.

24. Ibid., 331.

Notes to Chapter 7

1. You can find this exercise—and many other useful teaching tools and key facts about inequality—in Chuck Collins and Felice Yeskel, *Economic Apartheid in America* (New York: New Press, 2005).

2. This argument is the one most widely discussed in the commentary on Piketty. It is laid out in detail in Part 3, focusing on both inequality in income and wealth.

3. Thomas Piketty, *Capital in the Twenty-First Century* (Cambridge, MA: Belknap, 2014), 264.

4. Ibid., 265.

5. Ibid., 263.

6. Ibid.

7. Ibid., 257–259.

8. Ibid., 259.

9. Ibid., 263.

10. To see what such a seminar might look like, see Charles Derber, *Marx's Ghost: Midnight Conversations on Changing the World* (Boulder, CO: Paradigm, 2011).

11. Piketty, *Capital*, 264.

12. Ibid., 265.

13. Ibid.

14. Marx's view of the relation of capitalism to feudalism generally suggests that it is a liberating movement from a caste to a class society. See Karl Marx and Frederick Engels, *The Communist Manifesto* (New York: Merlin, 1998 reprint).

15. Piketty makes this argument, in several different ways, throughout his work, with the first account being on pp. 22–27.

16. See the critique in James K. Galbraith, "*Kapital* in the Twenty-First Century?," *Dissent*, Spring 2014, http://www.dissentmagazine.org/article/kapital-for-the-twenty-first-century. The main assault on the data after the book came out was issued with fanfare by Chris Giles, chief economics editor of the *Financial Times*. See Chris Giles, "Piketty Findings Undercut by Errors," *Financial Times*, May 23, 2014, http://www.ft.com/cms/s/2/e1f343ca-e281-11e3 -89fd-00144feabdc0.html#axzz39qqQrH43. Piketty responded persuasively, according to most analysts, debunking the *Financial Times* critique. See Thomas Piketty, "Technical Appendix of the Book: Addendum: Response to FT," May 18, 2014, http://piketty.pse.ens.fr/files/capital21c/en/Piketty2014TechnicalAppendixResponsetoFT.pdf.

17. Ibid.

18. Piketty introduces Kuznets and his arguments early on, immediately refuting his central premise. Piketty, *Capital*, 13–15.

19. Ibid.

20. $R > g$ is first introduced by Piketty on p. 25. It is then discussed throughout the book, but the basic argument is summarized on pp. 25–27.

21. Ibid., 26.

22. Ibid., 27.

23. Ibid.

24. David Harvey, "Afterthoughts on Piketty's Capital," Reading Marx's Capital with David Harvey, May 5, 2014, http://davidharvey.org/2014/05/afterthoughts-pikettys-capital/; Galbraith, "*Kapital* in the Twenty-First Century?"

25. Harvey, "Afterthoughts on Piketty's Capital."

26. This quote is taken from my interview with Piketty, cited in prior notes.

27. Piketty, *Capital*, 330ff.

28. Marx and Engels, *The Communist Manifesto*.

29. See Alvin Gouldner, *The Two Marxisms* (New York: Oxford University Press, 1964). See also Charles Derber and Yale Magrass, *Capitalism: Should You Buy It? An Invitation to Political Economy* (Boulder, CO: Paradigm, 2014), chapters 1 and 2.

30. Piketty, *Capital*, 27.

Notes to Chapter 8

1. Charles Derber and Yale Magrass, *Capitalism: Should You Buy It? An Invitation to Political Economy* (Boulder, CO: Paradigm, 2014), chapters 1–2.

2. Ibid., chapter 3.

3. Thomas Piketty, *Capital in the Twenty-First Century* (Cambridge, MA: Belknap, 2014), 419ff.

4. Max Weber, *The Protestant Ethic and the Spirit of Capitalism* (New York: Merchant, 2013 reprint).

5. Paul Ryan, cited in Hunter Stuart and Saki Knafu, "Paul Ryan Looks at the Poor, Sees 'Takers,'" *Huffington Post*, October 26, 2012.

6. Sherrie D. Larch, "Televangelism, the Gospel of Prosperity," http://larchinski .hubpages.com/hub/TelevangelismSDLarch.

7. Derber and Magrass, *Capitalism*, chapters 3 and 6.

8. See, for example, the account of Rastignac's dilemma (pp. 238–242) in Balzac's *Pere Goriot*, who was doomed to a middling income if he worked endlessly hard and would be far wiser to marry upward into wealth, the literary entry into the centrality of inherited wealth in Europe's Belle Époque.

9. Piketty, *Capital*, 331–333.

10. Ibid., 439.

11. Ibid., 441.

12. Ibid., 332–334.

13. Ibid., 334.

14. Ibid., 331.

15. Ibid.

16. Ibid.

17. See Charles Derber, *Hidden Power: What You Need to Know to Save Our Democracy* (San Francisco: Berrett-Koelhler, 2005).

18. Derber and Magrass, *Capitalism*, chapters 5 and 6.

19. Piketty, *Capital*, 332.

20. Ibid.

21. Ibid., 308–313.

Notes to Chapter 9

1. "Most See Inequality Growing, but Partisans Differ Over Solutions: 54 Percent Favor Taxing the Wealthy to Expand Aid to the Poor," Pew Research Center, January 23, 2014, http://www.people-press.org/2014/01/23/most-see-inequality-growing-but-partisans-differ-over-solutions/.

2. Ibid.

3. Jason DeParle, "Harder to Rise from Lower Rungs," *New York Times*, January 4, 2012, http://www.nytimes.com/2012/01/05/us/harder-for-americans-to-rise-from-lower-rungs.

4. Ibid.

5. Ibid.

6. Ibid.

7. Thomas Piketty, *Capital in the Twenty-First Century* (Cambridge, MA: Belknap, 2014), 484.

8. Raj Chetty, Nathaniel Hendren, Patrick Kline, Emmanuel Saez, and Nichalas Turner, "Is the United States Still a Land of Opportunity? Recent Trends in Intergenerational Mobility," Working Paper 19844, National Bureau of Economic Research, January 2014, http://www.equality-of-opportunity.org/files/mobility_trends.pdf.

9. Piketty references questions and data about lifetime income mobility on pp. 299–300.

10. Ibid., 22.

11. Ibid., 484.

12. Ibid.

13. Ibid.

14. Ibid., 485.

15. Ibid.

16. Ibid.

17. Ibid.

18. Ibid., 486–487.

19. I develop this argument at length in Charles Derber and Yale Magrass, *The Surplus American: How the 1% Is Making Us Redundant* (Boulder, CO: Paradigm, 2012).

20. Charles Derber, *Sociopathic Society: A People's Sociology of the United States* (Boulder, CO: Paradigm, 2013), especially chapter 1. See also Charles Derber, *The Wilding of America*, 6th ed. (New York: Worth and Macmillan, 2015).

21. Piketty, *Capital*, 238–242.

22. Ibid., 27.

23. Ibid., 515–516.

24. This view of the compatibility of capitalism with the American Dream, based on prospects of political intervention to reduce inequality and increase mobility, is shared not only by Piketty in parts of his book, but more emphatically by Joseph Stiglitz, "Inequality Is not Inevitable," Opinionator, *New York Times*, June 27, 2014, http://opinionator.blogs.nytimes.com/author/joseph-e-stiglitz/; Robert Reich, *Aftershock: The Next Economy and America's Future* (New York: Vintage, 2010); and Paul Krugman, *End This Depression Now* (New York: W. W. Norton, 2013).

25. For a brief review of these "new economy" schools, see Charles Derber and Yale Magrass, *Capitalism: Should You Buy It? An Invitation to Political Economy* (Boulder, CO: Paradigm, 2014), chapter 14.

26. Ibid., chapter 5.

27. Ibid., chapters 5 and 6.

28. Ibid., chapter 5.

29. Thomas Frank, *What's the Matter with Kansas? How Conservatives Won the Heart of America* (New York: Holt, 2005).

Notes to Chapter 10

1. Thomas Piketty, *Capital in the Twenty-First Century* (Cambridge, MA: Belknap, 2014), 14–15.

2. While Keynesians who discuss US militarism are rare, many neo-Marxist political economists do: Why the difference? Such analyses often lead to systemic critiques of capitalism, and Keynesians embrace the capitalist system while neo-Marxists reject it. It is thus consistent with the fundamental ideological stances of both schools that they take up the subjects on war that they do. Keynes himself, of course, was deeply concerned about war and economics, predicting that the harsh war reparations of World War I would lead to economic collapse and another great war. But he did not discuss Western militarism or imperialism in any depth. The neo-Marxists who discuss militarism and imperialism go back to Lenin; see Vladimir Lenin, *Imperialism: The Highest Stage of Capitalism* (New York: International Publishers, 1969). See

also Harry Magdoff, *The Age of Imperialism: The Economics of US Foreign Policy* (New York: Monthly Review Press, 2000).

3. The most important analyst of US foreign policy and US imperialism is Noam Chomsky. For a relatively recent example of his work, see Chomsky, *Hopes and Prospects* (Boston: Haymarket, 2010). See also Chomsky, *Understanding Power: The Indispensable Chomsky* (New York: New Press, 2002). For a different critique of US militarism, see Andrew Bacevich, *The New American Militarism* (New York: Oxford, 2013). See also Bacevich, *Washington Rules: America's Path to Permanent War* (New York: Metropolitan, 2011).

4. Piketty, *Capital*, 146ff.

5. Ibid., 148.

6. Ibid.

7. Ibid., 149.

8. Ibid.

9. Ibid., 507.

10. Charles Derber and Yale Magrass, *Capitalism: Should You Buy It? An Invitation to Political Economy* (Boulder, CO: Paradigm, 2014), chapter 4.

11. Ibid.

12. Ibid.

13. Ibid. See also Charles Derber, *Regime Change Begins at Home: Freeing America from Corporate Rule* (San Francisco: Berrett-Koehler, 2004)

14. For a summary and critique of those concluding, based on World War II, that war is good for the economy, see Seymour Melman, *The Permanent War Economy* (New York: Simon and Schuster, 1974).

15. Noam Chomsky, *Neoliberalism and Global Order* (San Francisco: Seven Stories, 2011). See also Andrew Bacevich, *The Limits of Power* (New York: Holt, 2009).

16. Derber and Magrass, *Capitalism*, chapter 4.

17. Ibid. See also Derber, *Regime Change Begins at Home.*

18. Noam Chomsky, *Neoliberalism and Global Order*; Joseph Stiglitz, *The Price of Inequality* (New York: W.W. Norton, 2013). See also Derber, *Regime Change Begins at Home*; and Chuck Collins, *99 to 1: How Wealth Inequality Is Wrecking the World and What We Can Do about It* (San Francisco: Berrett-Koehler, 2012).

19. Stiglitz, *The Price of Inequality*; Derber, *Regime Change Begins at Home.* See also Charles Derber, *Corporation Nation* (New York: St. Martin's, 2000).

20. Derber, *Regime Change Begins at Home.*

21. Stiglitz, *The Price of Inequality.*

22. Collins, *99 to 1.*

23. Derber and Magrass, *Capitalism*, chapter 4.

Notes to Chapter 11

1. Thomas Piketty, *Capital in the Twenty-First Century* (Cambridge, MA: Belknap, 2014), 567.

2. Ibid., 567–569.

3. Ibid.

4. Ibid., 567.

5. Ibid., 95.

6. Ibid.

7. Juliet Schor, *True Wealth* (New York: Penguin, 2011); John Bellamy Foster, *The Ecological Rift* (New York: Monthly Review Press, 2011). See also John Bellmay Foster, "Occupy Denialism; Toward Ecological and Social Revolution," Znet, November 12, 2011.

8. Hermann Daly, *Beyond Growth* (Boston: Beacon, 1997).

9. Bill McKibben, *Eaarth: Making a Life on a Tough New Planet* (New York: St. Martin's, 2011).

10. Schor, *True Wealth*. See also Charles Derber and Yale Magrass, *Capitalism: Should You Buy It? An Invitation to Political Economy* (Boulder, CO: Paradigm, 2014), chapter 10; and Foster, "Occupy Denialism."

11. Charles Derber, *Greed to Green: Solving Climate Change and Remaking the Economy* (Boulder, CO: Paradigm, 2010).

12. For a reconsideration of globalization that would permit equitable growth consistent with reducing climate change, see Joseph Stiglitz, *Globalization and Its Discontents* (New York: W.W. Norton, 2003).

13. Derber, *Greed to Green*.

14. Foster, *The Ecological Rift*. See also John Bellamy Foster, *Ecology against Capitalism* (New York: Monthly Review Press, 2002); *Marx's Ecology: Materialism and Nature* (New York: Monthly Review Press, 2000); and "Occupy Denialism."

15. Our most important critic of mass consumerism, written from the perspective of climate change concerns. See especially Schor, *True Wealth*. See also Juliet Schor, *Born to Buy* (New York: Scribner, 2005).

16. Schor, *True Wealth*. See also McKibben, *Eaarth*.

17. Piketty, *Capital*, 494.

18. Karl Marx, *Das Kapital*, chapter 1. See also Charles Derber, *Marx's Ghost: Midnight Conversations on Changing the World* (Boulder, CO: Paradigm, 2011).

19. Schor, *True Wealth*; McKibben, *Eaarth*; Derber, *Greed to Green*.

20. Thorstein Veblen, *The Theory of the Leisure Class* (New York: Macmillan, 1899).

21. Piketty, *Capital*, 621n48.

22. Matthew Josephson, *The Robber Barons* (New York: Mariner, 1962).

23. For a discussion of cultural capital, and its relation to conspicuous consumption, see Pierre Bordieu, *Distinction: A Social Critique of the Judgment of Taste* (Cambridge, MA: Harvard University Press, 1984).

24. Piketty, *Capital*, 32.

25. Derber, *Greed to Green*.

26. Schor, *True Wealth*. See also Gar Alperovitz, "The Rise of the 'New Economy' Movement," *Huffington Post*, May, 22, 2012, http://www.huffingtonpost.com/gar-alperovitz/the-rise -of-the-new-econo_b_1532549.html. See also Gar Alperovitz, *What Then Must We Do?* (White River Junction, VT: Chelsea Green, 2013); and Derber and Magrass, *Capitalism*, chapter 14.

27. This was the argument first made so powerfully in mid-twentieth-century society by John Kenneth Galbraith, *The Affluent Society* (New York: Mariner, 1998). See also Charles Derber and June Sekera, "An Invisible Crisis: We Are Suffering from a Growing Public Goods Deficit," *Boston Globe*, January 22, 2014, http://www.bostonglobe.com/opinion/2014/01/22 /the-hidden-deficit/LMvPwkE9tPmOQcezlCTFjM/story.html.

Notes to *Reading Capital in the Anthropocene*

1. Stephen A. Marglin and Juliet B. Schor, *The Golden Age of Capitalism: Reinterpreting the Postwar Experience* (Oxford: Clarendon Press, 1989).

2. For a discussion and estimates of the stranded assets of fossil fuel companies, see Carbon Tracker Initiative, "Unburnable Carbon: Wasted Capital and Stranded Assets," http://www .lse.ac.uk/GranthamInstitute/wp-content/uploads/2014/02/PB-unburnable-carbon-2013-wasted -capital-stranded-assets.pdf.

Notes to Chapter 12

1. Thomas Piketty, *Capital in the Twenty-First Century* (Cambridge, MA: Belknap, 2014), 1.

2. This is the central premise of neoclassical economics, developed most famously by Milton Friedman, *Capitalism and Democracy*: Fortieth Anniversary Edition (Chicago: University of Chicago Press, 2002).

3. Piketty, *Capital*, 573.

4. Ibid., 422ff.

5. Ibid., 424.

6. Ibid.

7. Ibid., 422.

8. Louis Brandeis, "Brainyquote," http://www.brainyquote.com/quotes/quotes/l/louisd-bra140392.html.

9. Piketty, *Capital*, 422.

10. Ibid.

11. See Friedman, *Capitalism and Democracy*. See also Charles Derber and Yale Magrass, *Capitalism: Should You Buy It? An Invitation to Political Economy* (Boulder, CO: Paradigm, 2014), chapters 3 and 7.

12. Karl Marx and Frederick Engels, *The Capitalist Manifesto* (New York: Merlin, 1998 reprint).

13. Derber and Magrass, *Capitalism*, chapters 5 and 7. See also ibid.

14. Derber and Magrass, *Capitalism*, chapters 5 and 7. See also Alvin Gouldner, *The Two Marxisms* (New York: Oxford University Press, 1964).

15. Piketty, *Capital*, 1.

16. Ibid.

17. Ibid., 422ff.

18. See his discussion of equal rights and the social state—or social democracy—in his chapter 13, pp. 471ff.

19. Friedman, *Capitalism and Democracy*; Derber and Magrass, *Capitalism*, chapters 3 and 7.

20. Ibid.

21. Piketty, *Capital*, 308ff.

22. Ibid., 331ff.

23. Ibid., 308ff.

24. Charles Derber, *Corporation Nation* (New York: St. Martin's, 2000); Derber and Magrass, *Capitalism*, chapters 5 and 7.

25. Paul Krugman, *End This Depression Now* (New York: W.W. Norton, 2013).

26. Ibid. See also Derber and Magrass, *Capitalism*, chapters 4 and 7.

27. C. Wright Mills, *The Power Elite* (New York: Oxford University Press, 1957); G. William Domhoff, *Who Rules America?* (New York: McGraw-Hill, 2009). See also Derber, *Corporation Nation*.

Notes to Chapter 13

1. Thomas Piketty, *Capital in the Twenty-First Century* (Cambridge, MA: Belknap, 2014), chapters 14–15.

2. Ibid., 474ff.

3. Ibid., 479.

4. Ibid., 479–480.

5. Ibid., 480.

6. Ibid.

7. Ibid.

8. Ibid.

9. Ibid., 481.

10. Ibid., 480.

11. Ibid.

12. Ibid., 482.

13. Ibid.

14. Ibid., 494.

15. Ibid., 495.

16. Ibid.,507–508.

17. Ibid., chapter 15.

18. Ibid., 528.

19. Ibid., 518–520.

20. Ibid., 518.

21. Ibid., 482.

22. Ibid., 483.

23. There is a long and growing literature critiquing the large corporate foundations as disguised ways of spreading corporate influence in the name of public advocacy. See, for example, William Domhoff, *Who Rules America?* (New York: McGraw-Hill, 2009).

24. Piketty, *Capital*, 483.

25. Ibid., 482–483.

26. Charles Derber, *Corporation Nation* (New York: St. Martin's, 2000), chapter 13.

27. Gar Alperovitz, *What Then Must We Do?* (White River Junction, VT: Chelsea Green, 2013).

Notes to *Thomas Piketty and Wealth Taxation in America*

1. Robert Lord, "Dr. King's Nightmare," Other Words, January 15, 2014, http://other words.org/dr-kings-nightmare-racial-wealth-gap-forbes400/.

2. Josh Bivens, "A Key Lesson from Piketty: You Can't Reverse Inequality or Provide Broad-Based Prosperity While Ignoring the Top 1 Percent," Working Economics Blog, Economic Policy Institute, April 17, 2014, http://www.epi.org/blog/key-lesson-piketty-reverse-inequality-provide.

3. "Does America Promote Mobility as Well as Other Nations?" Pew Charitable Trusts, Economic Mobility Project, November 2011, page 4 of summary, http://www.pewstates.org /uploadedFiles/PCS_Assets/2011/CRITA_FINAL(1).pdf.

4. Research work by Miles Corak in Timothy M. Smeeding, Robert Erikson, and Markus Jantti, editors, *Persistence, Privilege, and Parenting: The Comparative Study of Intergenerational Mobility* (New York: Russell Sage Foundation, 2011). Also see blog interview with Corak at http://www.russellsage.org/blog/comparing-economic-mobility-canada-and-america-interview -miles-corak.

5. "Income Inequality," Institute for Policy Studies, http://www.inequality.org.

6. Research on intergenerational wealth transfers including a Boston College study as well as the study "The Greater Wealth Transfer," *Accenture*, June 2012. Also see http://www .bc.edu/content/dam/files/research_sites/cwp/pdf/Wealth%20Press%20Release%205.28-9 .pdf, and http://nypost.com/2014/06/22/top-1-percent-spreading-nearly-60t-in-assets-to-heirs -charities/.

7. For a full history of the estate tax, see Bill H. Gates Sr. and Chuck Collins, *Wealth and Our Commonwealth: Why America Should Tax Accumulated Fortunes* (Boston: Beacon Press, 2003).

8. Chuck Collins, "Fixing and Expanding the Estate Tax: Intervening to Reduce Wealth Inequality," April 15, 2014, http://www.ips-dc.org/fixing_expanding_the_estate_tax/.

9. Zach Mider, "Accidental Tax Break Saves Wealthiest Americans $100 Billion," *Bloomberg News*, December 17, 2013, http://www.bloomberg.com/news/2013-12-17/accidental -tax-break-saves-wealthiest-americans-100-billion.html.

10. See Chuck Collins, "Close the Billionaire Loophole," April 15, 2014, https://www .commondreams.org/view/2014/04/15.

11. Chuck Collins, Conor Kenny, Lee Farris, and Lincoln Taylor, "Spending Millions to Save Billions: The Campaign of the Super Wealthy to Kill the Estate Tax," Public Citizen & United for a Fair Economy, April 2006, http://www.citizen.org/documents/EstateTaxFinal.pdf.

12. See Bill Gates Sr. and Chuck Collins, "A GI Bill for the Next Generation," *Houston Chronicle*, June 22, 2004, http://www.chron.com/opinion/outlook/article/It-s-time-for-a-GI -Bill-for-the-next-generation-1504916.php.

13. Rohit Chopra, "Student Debt Swells, Federal Loans Now Top a Trillion," Consumer Financial Protection Bureau, July 17, 2013.

14. "Examining the Mismanagement of the Student Loan Rehabilitation Process," Testimony of James W. Runcie, Chief Operating Officer Federal Student Aid at US Department of Education, Hearing before Subcommittee on Higher Education and Workforce Training, House Education and the Workforce Committee, March 12, 2014, http://docs.house.gov /meetings/ED/ED13/20140312/101885/HHRG-113-ED13-Wstate-RuncieJ-20140312.pdf.

15. Richard Fry, "A Record One-in-Five Households Now Owe Student Loan Debt: Burden Greatest on Young, Poor." *Pew Research: Social and Demographic Trends.* September 26, 2012.

16. Jesse Rothstein and Cecilia Elena Rouse, "Constrained after College: Student Loans and Early Career Occupational Choices," National Bureau of Economic Research, NBER Working Paper No. 13117, May 2007.

17. Brent W. Ambrose, Larry Cordell, and Shuwei Ma, "The Impact of Student Loan Debt on Small Business Formation." Economic Working Paper. March 29, 2014, available at Social Science Research Network.

18. Dora Gicheva, "Does the Student-Loan Burden Weigh into the Decision to Start a Family?" University of North Carolina at Greensboro, March 2011.

19. Jennifer M. Shand, "The Impact of Early-Life Debt on the Homeownership Rates of Young Households: An Empirical Investigation," Federal Deposit Insurance Corporation (FDIC), November 2007.

20. Thomas G. Mortenson, "State Funding: A Race to the Bottom," American Council on Education, Winter 2012, http://www.acenet.edu/the-presidency/columns-and-features /Pages/state-funding-a-race-to-the-bottom.aspx.

21. Phil Oliff, Vincent Palacios, Ingrid Johnson, and Michael Leachman, "Recent Deep State Higher Education Cuts May Harm Students and the Economy for Years to Come," Center on Budget and Policy Priorities, March 19, 2013, http://www.cbpp.org/cms/index .cfm?fa=view&id=3927.

22. John Quinterno, "The Great Cost Shift: How Higher Education Cuts Undermine Us All," *Demos*, October 2012.

23. Ibid.

24. Martha J. Bailey and Susan M. Dynarski, "Gains and Gaps: Changing Inequality in US College Entry and Completion," NBER Working Paper No. 17633. See digest by Laurent Belsie at http://www.nber.org/papers/w17633.pdf.

25. Research by Caroline M. Hoxby of Stanford and Christopher Avery of Harvard, as cited in David Leonardt, "Better Colleges Failing to Lure Strivers," *New York Times*, March 16, 2013.

26. Heidi Shierholz and Lawrence Mishel, "A Decade of Flat Wages the Key Barrier to Shared Prosperity and a Rising Middle Class," Economic Policy Institute. August 21, 2013.

27. Quinterno, "The Great Cost Shift."

28. Robert Hiltonsmith and Tamara Draut, "The Great Cost Shift Continues: State Higher Education Funding after the Recession," *Demos*, March 2014.

29. John R. Burbank and Marilyn Watkins, "Washington's Estate Tax: Revenue for Higher Education and Early Learning," Economic Opportunity Institute, February 24, 2010, www.research.policyarchive.org/95802.pdf.

Notes to Chapter 14

1. Elizabeth Warren, *A Fighting Chance* (New York: Metropolitan, 2014).

2. See also Robert Reich, *Beyond Outrage* (New York: Vintage, 2012).

3. Robert Kuttner, "What Piketty Leaves Out," *American Prospect*, April 2014, http://prospect.org/article/what-piketty-leaves-out. See also Tom Frank, "The Problem with Thomas Piketty."

4. See Piketty's response to Robert Kuttner in Kuttner's review, "What Piketty Leaves Out."

5. Thomas Piketty, *Capital in the Twenty-First Century* (Cambridge, MA: Belknap, 2014), 469ff.

6. I have outlined the argument for this kind of populist agenda in several of my books, including Derber, *Corporation Nation: How Corporations Are Taking Over Our Lives—and What We Can Do about It* (New York: St. Martin's, 2000); *Hidden Power: What You Need to Know to Save Our Democracy* (San Francisco: Berrett-Koehler, 2005); *Greed to Green: Solving Climate Change and Remaking the Economy* (Boulder, CO: Paradigm, 2010); *Marx's Ghost: Midnight Conversations on Changing the World* (Boulder, CO: Paradigm, 2011); *Sociopathic Society: A People's Sociology of the United States* (Boulder, CO: Paradigm, 2013); and with Yale Magrass, *The Surplus American: How the 1% Is Making Us Redundant* (Boulder, CO: Paradigm, 2012); and (also with Magrass) *Capitalism: Should You Buy It? An Invitation to Political Economy* (Boulder, CO: Paradigm, 2014).

7. Derber, *Hidden Power.*

8. Regarding the New Deal era, see especially William Domhoff, *The Myth of Liberal Ascendancy* (Boulder, CO: Paradigm, 2013). See also Domhoff, *Who Rules America?* (New York: McGraw-Hill, 2013); and Domhoff, *The Higher Circles* (New York: Vintage, 1971).

9. Derber, *Hidden Power.*

10. Howard Zinn, *A People's History of the United States* (New York: Harper Perennial, 2005).

11. Piketty, *Capital,* 574.

12. Derber, *Corporation Nation.* See also Derber, *Sociopathic Society.*

13. Derber, *Hidden Power*; Derber, *Corporation Nation*; Derber, *Sociopathic Society.*

14. Pew Research Center, "Capitalism Not so Positive, Socialism Not so Negative," May 4, 2010, *http://www.people-press.org/2010/05/04/socialism-not-so-negative-capitalism-not-so-positive/.* For a discussion of these poll data, see Charles Derber, "Big Surprises in Recent Polls," Common Dreams, May 18, 2010, http://www.commondreams.org/views/2010/05/18/capitalism-big-surprises-recent-polls.

15. A classic treatment of this is Stanley Aronowitz, *False Promises* (Durham, NC: Duke University Press, 1991).

INDEX

Academic labor market, 74–75

Accumulation, class system based on, 24–25

Afghanistan, war in, 93

African Americans: cultural caste, 34

Air-traffic control union, 94

Alger, Horatio, 41–42

Alperovitz, Gar, 131

American Dream. *See* Mobility

American Revolution, 124–125

American Taxpayer Relief Act (ATRA), 136

Anthropocene epoch, 109

Aristocracy: bourgeoisie envying and emulating, 42; bourgeoisie overthrow of, 39–40; cultural capital, 43–44; patrimonial capitalism, 71. *See also* Feudalism

Austen, Jane: capitalist-aristocrat interactions, 40–41; patrimonial capitalism, 71–72; social groupings of Piketty class distinctions, 26–27. *See also* Belle Époque capitalism; Gilded Age

Autocracy: capitalism replacing democracy with, 143–144; caste system as, 115

Baby bonds, 137

Balanced growth, xxv

Balzac, Honore de: patrimonial capitalism, 71–72; social groupings of Piketty class distinctions, 26–27; social mobility, 27, 161(n8). *See also* Belle Époque capitalism; Gilded Age

Banking industry: social class behavior of the 1%, 26

Belle Époque capitalism: caste and caste ideology, 32–33; meritocracy, 76–77; patrimonial capitalism, 71. *See also* Gilded Age

Bettencourt, Liliane, 72

Billionaire loopholes in the estate tax, 136

Biological caste, xiii–xiv, 25, 29–30, 33, 36, 150–152

Bohemian groves, 33

Bourdieu, Pierre, 43–44, 105

Bourgeoisie: envying and emulating the aristocracy, 42; as outcastes, 39; overthrow of the aristocracy, 39–40

Brandeis, Louis, 114

Bridgeland, John, 79

Britain: bourgeoisie revolutions, 39–40; destruction of capital during wars, 90; taxation of the wealthy, 127. *See also* Gilded Age

Bubbles, 24

Bush, George H. W., 44

Bush, George W., 44, 93–94

Capital: the anatomy of capital and wealth, xxii; climate change leading to loss of, 110–112; composition of, xxiv; defining, xx; defining national income, xxi–xxii; democratic control of, 123–124, 126–131, 143–144, 148; destruction of capital during wars, 90; extreme concentration of, 57–58;

ABOUT THE AUTHOR

Charles Derber, Professor of Sociology at Boston College, has written for *Newsday, Newsweek, Business Week, Time,* the *Christian Science Monitor,* and other magazines. He speaks frequently on National Public Radio, talk radio, and television. His most recent book is *Capitalism: Should You Buy It? An Invitation to Political Economy* (Paradigm 2014).